Horse Training How-To from Horsemanship101.com

What Is Wrong with My Horse?

Fixing Problems DIY & Step-by-Step

"What Is Wrong with My Horse?"
by Keith Hosman
ISBN: 1477697713
ISBN-13: 978-1477697719

Copyright (C) 2012-2015
by Keith Hosman, PO Box 31, Utopia, TX 78884 USA
All rights reserved. No part of this publication may be reproduced, stored in a retrieval system, or transmitted, in any form or by any means, electronic, mechanical photocopying, recording, or otherwise, without the prior written permission of the publisher.

Please note: The information appearing in this publication is presented for educational purposes only. In no case shall the publishers or authors be held responsible for any use readers may choose to make, or not to make, of this information.

Keith Hosman
horsemanship101.com
PO Box 31
Utopia, TX 78884 USA

020714

Horse Training How-To from Horsemanship101.com

What Is Wrong with My Horse?

Fixing Problems DIY & Step-by-Step

by John Lyons Certified Trainer Keith Hosman

Table of Contents

Preface 9
Use this handbook to "fix your horse for good."

Section I: Fear, In All Its Forms
How your horse gets scared determines how we go about fixing it

Retraining the Flighty or Bratty Horse 13
Horses are herd animals and instinct tells them that there's gotta be a boss. If it's not you, it's gotta be them. Here's how to get and maintain control.

Whoever Moves First Loses (Or, "How to Get Respect") 19
Here's something you can do to take back (sustain, or solidify) your rightful spot as leader in your "herd of two."

"I'm Scared of My Horse, Please Help" (The Intimidating Horse) 28
Is your horse the boss of you? Turn things around by learning to spot the moments when your horse takes control.

Despooking: Scary Things 34
Sack out and desensitize your horse to scary objects - like your hands, tack and everyday equipment.

Despooking: Scary Moments 44
Here's how to teach your horse to contain himself (and thus, keep you safe) when something scary pops out of nowhere.

Despooking: Scary Places 50
Does you horse turn into a basket case every single solitary time he gets near the same darn spot on the trail or seemingly innocent patch of arena dirt? Here's your fix.

Despooking: Scary 'Away' Places.....................55
When your horse only turns into a freakzoid when you've trailered to a distant location - like a show - here's what to do.

Say Good-Bye to Mr. Jiggy 61
Here we'll learn to relax and slow a high horse with a method so simple that it only has one step.

How to Slow Down Your Too-Fast Horse........67
If you have problems with your horse getting "higher and higher" -- or need a way to slow a fast one down -- then this is for you.

Calm Down Now... 72
Nature placed an On/Off switch onto each horse. This exercise gives you the "flip switch."

Section II: Keeping Your Horse On the Straight and Narrow
What you do today determines the horse you'll ride tomorrow.

Perfect the First Time 83
If you're guilty of being a bit heavy-handed (as evidenced by a stiff-as-a-statue horse) here's a Top Five Horse Training Concept that will soften your horse fast.

6 Easy Ways to Improve Your Training............85
Six horse training tips, each designed to simplify your training and make big changes fast

Rider Checklists 92
Here are 3 "Rider Checklists." Together, they'll keep you safer - and accelerate your training to boot.

The First Thing I Do 99
Here's the first thing you should do with your horse today - and with any horse that's "new to you."

When You Get On, Do This First 106
Here's one small thing you can do to keep your horse's attitude in check - and prevent mount-up problems from taking root.

Is My Horse Hard to Train... Because of His Feet? 108
If your horse stumbles, cranes his head to the ground, takes halting steps, doesn't want to "move out," or has grown irritable, it might be that his feet are hurting him. Here's how to tell.

Section III: Overt Vices
Here's how to fix some of the most common problems you might face with your horse: Easy, objective, step-by-step

Horses That Bite 115
Biting is the worst vice your horse can have. It's more dangerous than bucking, than rearing, than kicking -- more dangerous than anything else you can name. Here's what to do.

Cinchy Horses 119
Here's an easy fix for horses that get cinchy or irritated when you tack up.

Horses That Won't Go 126
Addressed here: Horses that stop moving and stubbornly refuse to take another step. Two things not addressed here (at least not in-depth or specifically): Horses that have gradually become "dead-sided" and crossing obstacles.

Leading Stubborn Horses 136
Learn a quick fix to get a horse moving again if he freezes up when being led -- with an eye toward lasting changes.

Picking Up Feet.. 143
Teaching your horse to lift its feet on command is actually much simpler than folks tend to want to make it. Here's how.

Books by This Author 150
Meet the Author... 151
Keith Hosman, John Lyons Certified Trainer

Preface

Use this handbook to "fix your horse for good."

This book is dedicated to every horse owner who has seriously considered leaving the gate open and spilling a trail of corn out to the highway. I've been there, my brothers and sisters. I feel your pain. Horses can be an amazing high - but can also drive ya nuts faster than you can say "Why would you do this to me when I pay all the bills?"

This book is also dedicated to all you folks who, new to horses, ignored all sensible advice and bought a young horse, figuring you could "learn together." Doubtless, you're starting to doubt the sanity of that decision... but relax, it's our little secret. Cram what you can of this material each night; amaze your friends in the morning.

Section I: The lion's share of challenges faced by riders and owners revolve around some form of "fear," the rider's - or the horse's. Here we deal with "fright" in it's myriad forms.

Section II: Neglect your lawn, get weeds. Neglect your car, break down. Neglect your horse... collect trips to the ER. Here's what you need to know to keep your horse tuned-up and out of trouble.

Section III: Find step-by-step fixes for the "most popular" (notice the quotes?) problems faced by horse owners.

You are a horse owner with problems. This is a book with solutions.

Good luck in your training!

Section I: Fear, In All Its Forms

How your horse gets scared determines how we go about fixing it

Retraining the Flighty or Bratty Horse

Horses are herd animals and instinct tells them that there's gotta be a boss. If it's not you, it's gotta be them. Here's how to get and maintain control.

Holding, reclaiming, or initially earning your horse's respect is a matter of keeping an eye out for moments when he tests your position as boss and taking action.

If you've got a flighty or bratty horse - or even a horse you feel might be testing your authority - do this: Put a halter on it and go for a walk (with you on the ground). Walk around, watching the horse's ears until they prick up and he turns his head to look at something. That movement right there is what we've been waiting for. Memorize what it looks like from the safety of the ground. Walk some more and really take in the very instant when your horse abruptly changes his focus to something "over there."

Child's play? Sure, but you'd be surprised how many out of control horses are ridden by people who have overlooked or didn't recognize the very moment they lost control. Whey they finally get dumped, they have no idea where the storm came from.

Now, take that a step farther: Move off and wait till you lose the horse's focus again. Be ready and the instant it happens begin waving both hands, call out, hop if you have to - but get his focus on you - GET BOTH EYES LOOKING AT YOU. He'll probably try to keep one eye on you and one on "the thing." (Odd how they can do that.) You want both eyes and you'll keep hopping till you get both.

Find something that seems to continually steal your horse's attention and use it to your advantage. Your horse will want to look at the bizarre object rather than you. Even if you get his attention, you'll quickly lose it when he looks back at the object. This is your big chance to be proactive and to start making a change. Do not let the horse tune in on anything except you by keeping him moving about, clap your hands, whatever, anytime he turns his attention away.

Stand there looking at him square in the eyes - relaxed, but waiting for him to mess up by looking away. The moment he does, get on his case like white on rice. Absolutely insist on having both eyes look at you until you signal with your body language (by turning away) that you're through. Sidestep around the horse in a circle and expect him to turn around, looking at you. He'll probably stop turning when you first begin, right about the time you get to his ribs area - but keep getting him "back on you" and soon enough he'll follow you in a complete circle.

At first, he may rock back away from you as he turns rather stiffly and awkwardly, if he turns at all. Given that, you'll know he's progressing when he seems to lean or creep forward continuously (even through his turns) and moves with the fluidity of a snake, bending his body like a banana - as opposed to turning stiffly like he's got a 2X4 stuck you know where. Help create this fluidity by continuing asking him to move a bit forward as he turns; do this by slightly backing away, drawing him toward you. That's what we want, fluid and forward. Keep at this until you get it.

Take note that in this training you are not to continually make a hub-bub regardless of what the horse is doing; you are only to make a ruckus when he turns his focus away. Until then, when he's "on you," you are to be relaxed.

Begin working to lighten the amount of pressure it takes to get and hold his attention. It shouldn't take much as he learns what you expect, but consciously work to lessen the effort required. When you first begin, it might take you jumping up and down or whirling the end of the lead rope at his posterior - but once he understands what you're after and that you'll not take "no" for an answer, you'll find that simply kissing to him or turning toward him will pull his focus back to you. You don't need to smack them to get and retain their attention. Just practice, thought, and persistence.

Gaining and holding his focus is key to being seen as leader. It is imperative that you retain this ground. Henceforth, you are to be a benevolent dictator. While you can hang out with your horse all day and he can simply munch grass, if your body language tells him that you need his focus, then get in the habit of expecting it immediately. Develop a zero tolerance for anything less. You know how you can't turn your back on the Queen of England in her presence? Your horse should start learning to treat you with the same deference. You know when somebody is addressing you and when they're ignoring you; it's no different with the horse.

This goes a long way to keeping your horse on the straight and narrow; it's work like this that keeps your horse controlled while your friend's horse goes bonkers. It's also how you indirectly solve (at least in large part) behavioral issues such as horses that bully you at feeding time, drag you on the lead line, run off as you remove the halter, or otherwise becomes a handful. In the horse's eyes, it says "If you wouldn't do it to your mother, don't do it to me." (See the chapter "Whoever Moves First, Loses" in Section I for more advice on "taking charge.")

Keep a lookout for any and all infractions. They snowball. Consider the horse that bites today for the first time. He didn't "just bite Sally out of the blue." That horse told her last week with his pinned ears that he was going to bite. He just didn't say when. She should have picked up on those pinned ears and done something immediately.

The horse that kicked us today barged past us at the feeding trough every day last week. The horse that just stepped on our feet pushed us with it's shoulder this morning. The horse that just bolted into the next county took eighteen hundred pounds of pressure - and thirty-two hundred yards - to stop last week. They all sent signals that danger lie ahead.

Maybe you don't think your horse ever sends a signal - he just gets "fed up" at some arbitrary point and begins bucking. Uh, guess what? He sends signals. The signals get broadcast in the moments, even days, preceding the buck. If it's a buck out of disrespect the signal could have been the horse freezing up, ignoring your cue to slow down or kicking the stall when you didn't move fast enough with the grain. Is it bucking caused by fear? Maybe the signal was throwing his shoulder into you as you led it past the scary garbage cans or a "near bolt" through the exit when some kid blew a whistle.

Fix your horse by first taking a step back and thinking about what precipitates its dangerous behavior. What transgression are we missing or ignoring? What snowball is rolling down hill, gaining size and strength?

When your horse freezes up and won't move or pins his ears or just plain looks belligerent, he's screaming "You are not the boss of me and I'll be pushed just so far!" Don't ignore these moments. Do something right away to let him know he really screwed up and that sort of behavior won't be tolerated. Put the horse to work intensely for twenty minutes doing any exercise you can think of. Show him the connection between poor behavior and additional workload, the connection between tranquility and proper manners.

Is your horse's neck stiff when you turn? He's telling you that when he gets ready to bolt or buck you don't have a chance. A neck that's stiff during times of peace will be rock solid in times of stress and the reins will mean nothing. Stop anything else you're doing and work to soften and relax your horse. (See "Say Good-Bye to Mr. Jiggy," Section I)

Have you decided that it's just easiest to let your horse have his way some days because it's either not worth the fight - or because he scares you? This is only going to get far, far worse. Never let your horse diss you; It's always worth the effort to discipline. (See "Scared of My Horse" & "Whoever Moves First, Loses," Section I)

Will the horse lower its head to the ground when you ask? If not, he's telling you that it'll fly up when he's agitated - and you won't have a prayer of bringing it down. (Think "rearing.") Teach it to drop its head on cue. (See "Calm Down Now," Section I)

Does he throw his shoulder into you as you lead him and bully ahead? He's telling you that he's going to make things very interesting when you get on his back and ask for something he's not keen on. Do the groundwork necessary to gain control over his hips and shoulders. (Leading Stubborn Horses) (Whoever Moves First Loses)

Does your horse see a rabbit and jump? What's gonna happen when it's a pack of barking dogs? Teach your horse to stand and face what scares him with an exercise known as "Spook in Place." (See "Despooking: Scary Moments," Section I)

Does your horse drive ya nuts because it only seems to get crazy when you're in the show pen or away from home? You'll use speed control to excise those demons of his under controlled circumstances in the chapter "Despooking: Scary 'Away' Places," (in Section I).

Remember that no single exercise or regimen will guarantee your horse in all situations. It will most likely take a mix of applied concepts and exercises. Training or re-training a horse is a matter of commanding respect and progressively building in layers of control. It takes time, thought, consistency and dedication - after all this is a living breathing animal we're talking about. It'll have good days and bad days and force you to adapt. It'll take awareness on your part, coupled with time, consistency and intense practice to build the control you need to more safely diffuse situations when they do occur - or avoid poor behavior entirely.

Whoever Moves First Loses (Or, "How to Get Respect")

Here's something you can do to take back (sustain, or solidify) your rightful spot as leader in your "herd of two."

Does your horse bang impatiently on the stall at feeding time? Or lead poorly or bite or buck or kick out during a speed transition or drop his head to eat grass or forget you exist when whinnying to his buddies or "get cinchy" or act the fool for the farrier...? Does your horse see you more as servant than lord of the manor?

Or maybe you're looking for some effective training to do on a rainy or wintery day? Maybe something you can teach in a barn aisle when somebody else is using the arena?

For those of you who answered "aye," I'm going to describe a test and then a fix for horses that fail the test. We'll diagnose just how much control we have versus what we think we have; wrest back control we might have unconsciously ceded, improve "manners," and boost our training in general. Some of you will test your horses, they'll pass and you can move on to something else. I hazard to guess, however, that the vast majority of you will find that a little tune up is necessary.

If your horse does something (to you) that he'd never ever do to his mother, you've got a respect issue on your hands. Each of the problems listed above comes from a horse that doesn't see you as boss. More importantly, these horses are owned by folks (that'd be you) who either don't realize the dynamics at play or understand full well but don't know what they can do about it. Simply put, starting here and now, you gotta reset that relationship; you get back to being the boss.

In the round pen, we gain respect by controlling the horse's direction, by not allowing him to stop moving, through speed control, etcetera. At feeding time we enforce respect by not allowing him to bully us. When leading we keep our positioning by demanding he be polite, backing him up or drilling on other ground work exercises if he crowds us. We maintain a zero tolerance policy and we do so because we know that it's the little things that add up to the total package. (Right?)

As obvious as this sounds, you'd be amazed how often somebody will ask (at a clinic) how to fix a behavioral issue -- and swear they've been strict with their horses -- and yet I can see several screaming signals from the horse that he's spoiled, spoiled, spoiled. The owner, no disrespect if I'm describing uh, you, is wholly oblivious.

There's a little something we can do to take back (sustain, or solidify) our rightful spot as leader and it comes down to a phenomena we often turn to in our training: The horse's belief that "Whoever causes the other to move is the boss." Watch a group of horses in the pasture. At feeding time you'll see that the boss mare can easily move the others away from the trough as she approaches. Granted, she's earned this respect by backing up the threats she makes today with kicks made yesterday -- but this underlying understanding is the point here. From today forward, each and every time she gets the other horse to move without lifting a finger, so to speak, she further cements an understanding of just who's calling the shots. "I don't get out of your way, you get out of mine." You can take a cue from nature by instituting a similar measure.

Four things to bear in mind as you practice this lesson, each critical to your success: First, if and whenever possible, use your body language to move the horse. Don't resort to physical force unless you absolutely positively have to. (Horses rarely resort to violence and manage to maintain harmony in their herd, yet we humans feel it imperative to swat, smack and spur incessantly -- a good thing to keep in mind. If they can do it, so can you.) Second, if the horse does ignore you, be quick with your fix. Don't allow even two seconds to pass before you enforce your request. Third, what we're looking for is for the horse to "yield his body," not for him to simply "walk away." Know the difference? Ambling away with his "back turned" is a metaphorical flipping of the bird. Stepping the hips away while keeping both eyes focused on us is respect. Be mindful of the very way he carries himself as you work with your horse. You may need to keep him moving around until he begins to show deference. Fourth, practice everything described here from both left and right sides of the horse.

So, let's test your pony to see if he reads our body language and dutifully moves away when cued. (And, if not, let's teach him to.) Halter your horse and, holding the lead rope in your left hand, approach his left rump. Be careful to apply zero pressure to the lead and walk as if the horse isn't there at an even speed. Kiss (saying, in essence, "move") as you approach. Whether logic says that the horse will accurately read the situation and take a step away or not, it is imperative that you believe that he will indeed move. Trust me, your thoughts very much affect your body language. If you take a hesitating step, that balk will say "I'm second-guessing myself, maybe I'm not in charge here" and the horse will happily stand rock solid.

Now, go back and reread that last paragraph. From what I've seen of riders/owners at my clinics, a great percentage of folks will stop moving when approaching their horses because logic tells them their horse isn't going to move. It is imperative that you learn to walk forthrightly and right "through" your horse. As easy a concept as this sounds, you'd be amazed at how people will balk and turn back to me "He's not moving. Wahhh." If this is you... MAKE HIM MOVE. This whole dance must be fluid with zero hesitation. You've got the lead rope in your hands, use it. Better, you've got the logic of foresight, use it. Kiss first to let him know you're coming -- and the very instant you think the horse might stall out, put pressure on his nose and ask the hip to move. If that doesn't do the trick, make his nose touch his hip. If that doesn't work hit him with your crop.

Now, an aside: When you jump in your car, you first turn on the engine, right? The horse is the same way. When simply standing there, hanging out or munching grass, he's "off." I don't expect him to start moving body parts when I enter the arena like some crazed French mime; I expect him to remain calm and to do as he likes until my stance or verbal cue tells him "move something" (as with that heads-up kiss above). At times, I can and should be able to work in his presence and he can and should stand or act as if I'm not there. That's fine and even necessary. But then, to wake him up, I "turn his key" by kissing, "Hello, I need something." Looking directly at your horse, kissing, walking and staring at his hip... these things combined send a pretty clear signal "Hey, get in gear and move your rear, sister." While the kiss is a wake-up call, your stare and movement signal what it is specifically that should move. (After I've got the horse listening I can (and do) expect him to move through that session based on my movements, sans kiss.)

Back to the task at hand... You've held the lead in your left hand and walked toward the hip (following your heads-up kiss and resolute walk). You've practiced enough that he understands your request and moves his hips away nicely. You've perfected it from both left and right sides. The next step is simply to remove the halter and work for the same results. Should he ignore your requests at this point, just wave your arms or the lead toward his hip. Should he run off, tell yourself you should have begun in a smaller pen. Fetch him and try again. If you have issues here, go back and practice more with the horse haltered, being especially careful to ask the horse to keep his two eyes on you as he moves off (this helps keep them near you and from "turning tail").

If the horse won't move or moves like he's got rocks in his pants: It might be because you're not reprimanding resolutely or It might mean you're waiting too long after making your request before backing it up with a reprimand, forcing the issue. Always, always, always make your request and then back it up decisively two beats later if he fails to move upon your initial request. Remember, it's 1) Kiss to say "I need something," 2) Walk at the spot that needs to move. 3) Back up your request with a little motivation if you need to.

Next, put the halter back on and capitalize on the improvement you've made by asking the horse to back away from you: Ask the hips to swing away and then one half beat before they stop moving walk toward the horse's shoulders or chest, suggesting "Back up." Be sure to make your "back" request before those hips come to a rest for the same reason that it's easier to push a car that's already moving than one that's not. Use inertia and work on your timing: You kiss, he steps the hips over, you walk at his chest/shoulder while putting light pressure on the lead rope to now say "Back up." Only ask for a step or two and if he does step back, great -- but immediately bring him forward or swing his hips and end on that. (Be careful not to stand in front of him when there's a chance he could walk over you.) Do not release (quit) until you feel less pressure from him through the lead rope. (That is, less pressure than the time before.) If need be, keep those hips swinging or the horse walking forward until he does lighten (you'll feel it through your hand). Do not release as he's moving backwards unless he's actually speeding up as you do so. Releasing as he starts to slow in his back up will cause him to move still slower; he may also begin leaning away from you, like a tree blown in the wind.

If he moves sluggishly: 1) You're allowing it. Send him a wake-up call by reacting in a big way. Slap your hands, snap your whip, etc. Remember, energy in, energy out. And / Or, 2) You're allowing those hips to come to a full rest before asking for the change of direction. Adjust your timing, asking for "back" a full beat or two earlier.

Two further remedies you might try: 1) Try backing at an angle (It causes him to lift his legs higher and thus more lightly) and/or 2) Reverse things: Ask him to move forward then back then forward again (still ending on forward). Swing the hips, then without hesitation, back away from him asking for "forward," then immediately ask for either the back up (if you can get it) or another swing of the hips (if you can't get "back"). Once again, finish with forward steps or hip disengagement. As long as you put energy into this and keep him moving, (and only release when he grows lighter through the lead), he'll grow lighter and lighter on his feet. Before you know it, he'll be skating any direction as if on ice. Stick with it and keep him moving; you'll have the back up in no time.

Throughout your practice, you'll want to continuously judge the horse's willingness by quantifying the amount of pressure he places on the lead rope in your hand. (If he's pulling on the lead, he's not working with you.) Release your pressure (on the lead directly or through your body positioning) when the horse relaxes and does as you ask -- and when you feel the pressure through the lead lessen. (Tip: Try releasing when you think the horse has the correct idea, as opposed to a beat later when he actually makes the step. He'll learn even faster.)

Note that when we first train the horse to back up, to walk forward, or to side pass away, we're only looking for it to take a few steps before releasing our pressure, ending our mini-lesson. (This is especially true later when you ride the horse.) Once the two of you are practiced, you can ask for it to walk or back clear across the arena -- but get good at two steps before asking for ten.

Finally, when your horse understands the "You move away based on my body language" theme, get the shoulders moving. You want the ability to walk toward the horse's shoulders and have him pivot away (on those back legs specifically). An example of why you would need this: You're leading the horse at his left shoulder. You notice a dollar bill on the ground, behind you and to your right. You should be able to simply veer to the right while the horse briefly halts and pivots away, allowing you to snatch up the money. (If he didn't "pivot," but rather just sort of meandered about, he'd end up blocking you.)

There are a couple of ways to get the shoulders moving away, but in this situation, let's make it happen by asking for "outside turns." Those of you skilled in the round pen methods of John Lyons will recognize the components. If you stand at the point of your horse's shoulder and walk "at his neck" as in that example, you may find that he simply blocks you. Instead, back away from the horse by 10 to 20 feet and ask him to turn away from you by waving your hands at his nearest shoulder and kissing, walking toward the shoulder staring at it, cracking your whip in that direction, whatever it takes to get him to move away from you through the shoulders. If you were in a round pen, this would be an "outside turn," as the horse is asked to turn away from the center of the pen, rather than toward it. Naturally, you'll want to practice this in an enclosed space. Practice asking him to turn "out" from both sides till proficient. As the partnership improves, begin creeping forward, making your requests from an ever-smaller distance. Before long, you should find that you only need to kiss, then walk toward the horse's shoulder/head/neck and he'll obligingly move off.

Whether you have issues riding, leading, feeding, or just plain "being near," you can often help yourself a great deal by teaching your horse respect. As stressed repeatedly, horses put great stock in the concept of "whoever controls the movements of the other is the boss" so practice the material described above and you'll find renewed willingness in all aspects of your training.

"I'm Scared of My Horse, Please Help" (The Intimidating Horse)

Is your horse the boss of you? Turn things around by learning to spot the moments when your horse takes control.

This chapter is for people with a horse that "turned into a brat" since they've owned it. It concerns itself with ground manners and the like -- it does not deal with riding issues (such as the easily spooked horse).

Would you like to walk out to the barn, have your horse turn to you with a smile and just hang out, best friends forever? Well, that's possible, but first...

First the hard medicine: If your horse has developed poor ground manners (pushiness, rudeness or especially dangerous vices such as kicking or biting) since you've been in charge... then you'll only fix it by realizing that you need to make a change yourself. Every contact we have with our horses teaches them something -- and your behavior has "trained" him to walk all over you. When the horse came to live with you he saw you as a blank slate. Would you be in charge -- or would he? He knows somebody's gotta be. Millions of years of "survival of the fittest" programmed him to believe that there's gotta be a boss. If you're not ready for the post, he'll assume it. But now, months or years after moving in, the horse looks at you and sees a giant sucker, with the Tootsie Pop wrapper and everything.

But, you say, I don't want to frighten my horse by being too tough. I prize our relationship and want him to learn to trust me. I want to bond and be friends and run through the fields bareback with my hair flowing...

Well, you can have a terrific relationship, but it takes respect -- and respect must be earned. Begin by realizing that you're the one paying the bills. And your horse is certainly "not the boss of you." You keep your horse, giving him the very best of care, but in return he works for you and has a job to do. He'd be more than happy to sit on the couch in front of the TV, barking out orders for you to bring him pop and sandwiches -- but it can't work like that. You have to go to work everyday; your horse has to go to work everyday. Typically horses work an hour or so daily while we slog through traffic before putting in our eight -- so our equine friends, even those in full training, have a pretty good deal.

Your horse's job is to turn and face you when you enter the stall, to remain still as you bridle or mount, to carry you down the trail and pick up a trot or lope when asked, to pick up the correct lead -- and so on.

But you've heard all this before, haven't you? Your horse is still a pain. Okay, I'll bottom line it: If you read article after article and still your horse remains incorrigible, find a pro. There's plenty of professional horse trainers out there. Trust me, we'd love to have your business. But, you say, I can't afford a trainer. No? Can you afford the hospital bill for a broken shoulder? And how much is your little finger worth? Keep a bratty horse long enough and you'll lose all ten of those digits. Horses don't wake up one day and realize they've been too hard on you, it's time for a truce. They get worse.

You'll know it's time for a professional if you have certain questions or thoughts. For instance, if you're thinking "Nobody can get in the pen with him, where do I start?" then a simple article won't suffice. Call a pro. Or, maybe you're new to horses entirely and you bought a green youngster figuring the two of you "could learn together" and now you're asking "Where do I start?" Call a pro.

For the rest of you, I'll list some specific examples and fixes -- but that's all they'll be, examples. For you to see positive changes, you'll need to tailor this material to your own situation, starting off by instituting a zero tolerance policy toward disrespect in all areas of your horse partnering. Begin by proactively looking for small transgressions: If you're reading this, those transgressions must be there.

The single biggest thing you can take from this material is simply this: Start recognizing those moments when you cede control to your horse; be attentive and pay attention to those little slights that signal a loss of control: An unwillingness to lead at the speed you choose, a head swinging wildly to neigh to a buddy, ears pinning, rushing you at feeding time, bolting off as you remove the halter. Be proactive. Be on the lookout for a horse that disrespects you and nip it in the bud.

When you put a halter on your horse, do you have to wrestle his head toward you or does the large muscle in his neck stay soft? Does he "just tolerate" you or stand politely? Be conscious of these things. Allowing these moments to compound is how we build monsters that chase us from the pen. If the little voice in you says your horse is overstepping his bounds, then do something about it. And don't over-think this. It's just common sense. The change comes not so much from "how" you fix his thinking but "when" you fix it.

(The correct answer is "right away.") Do what it takes to get the horse to wake up and pay you the attention you're due (as the man or woman paying all the bills, for goodness sake). In these cases mentioned, it might be a matter of putting pressure on the lead till the horse relaxes and drops his neck, then releasing and petting. Maybe it's a matter of clapping your hands and getting the horse to look at you with two eyes. Maybe the answer is to simply get the horse to practice backing up or disengaging his hips (by directing his head towards his hip). It's not what you do, it's that you do do something -- and that you do it right away.

I could give you specific fixes for a horse that's hard to halter, head shy, doesn't keep up with you as you walk, etc. -- but those are each topics in their own right, and not what I want you to be learning here. What I want you to be learning is "Oh, that's when and why my horse is turning into a rude son of a gun." That simple realization will have profound effects on the relationship you share with your horse. Creating "behavior boundaries" for your horse is how you gain respect, it's the key to making horse keeping fun.

Let's try feeding your horse. Pour the grain out and be conscious of whether or not you cease to exist to the horse the moment he spots the food. Does he bull past as if you just disappeared? Maybe he pushes you rudely with his head? Do what my mother would do if I tried that at the dinner table as a kid: Go crazy. Let the horse know the very moment you suspect you've been treated rudely that those sorts of manners will not be tolerated. Scream, clap your hands, jump up and down, throw the bucket at him. He can wait to eat till he pays you homage, thank you very much. Let him know he'll not survive the next transgression -- and be quick about it. Remember, you only have three seconds to make the correction -- else the horse won't make the connection between mistake and your cursing. He'll just think you're odd. Also, anytime you make a correction, be sure to bring yourself back to neutral immediately.

Try walking around the paddock. Does he crane his neck to whinny to a nearby buddy, ignoring your request to keep walking ahead? Improve his attention span by improving his performance: Practice moving his shoulders or dropping his head and backing for twenty minutes. Does he keep throwing that nearest shoulder at you, threatening to run you over? Ask him to step those shoulders to his left and right for awhile. Be ready with your fixes because small infractions add up to one large dangerous horse. When your horse plants himself and refuses to take another step, make his nose touch his butt with a good swift pull on that lead line. Maybe snap his rear with the end of the lead. Scream if you have to, but get him moving. Taking his nose to his rear will move that shoulder safely away; it'll wake him up; it'll put you back in charge. (Put a bridle with a snaffle bit in his mouth for these exercises if you find the horse overpowering you when outfitted in just the halter.) Next, clap, dance or scream obscenities until you get the horse to look at you with two eyes. When you're ready, walk on, prepared to deliver unto the horse the wrath of seven maniacal tigers, should he pull that again. Let him know that you're the biggest bull in the barn, a bull that's totally relaxed and cheery if everyone follows the rules.

A common question is "Won't my horse start fearing me?" "Won't I jeopardize any existing good will that might exist if I get on his case?" Answer: Not if you're cut and dried about your fixes. Horses aren't stupid and they're fine with benevolent dictators. Be fair and consistent with your actions and they'll hand you respect.

Let them know that a bad attitude will not be tolerated -- and then you relax. Or, overlook these things, allow them to fester, and find yourself on the losing end.

Despooking: Scary Things

Sack out and desensitize your horse to scary objects - like your hands, tack and everyday equipment.

"Sacking out" is a horseman's way of saying "get the horse used to" everyday objects that it comes into contact with, objects like your hands, the lariat, lead rope, saddle, or halter. It's typically reserved for foals or young horses being readied for first-time saddling - but any skittish horse will benefit. You'd want to put your horse through this regimen regardless of age or background if it spooks at your unexpected touch, to having its head or legs handled, to something tied to the saddle bumping its sides, etcetera, etcetera.

The work in this chapter is specifically used to desensitize your horse to common objects that it might come into contact with regularly (again, like your hands or tack). We can't desensitize the horse to every object in the world that it might run into, however, so "uncommon objects that may or may not touch are horses" are dealt with in another way. To prepare your horse for "out of the blue" scary situations, including moments when an "object" might pop up (like a blowing grocery bag, gun shot, or barking dog), see the chapter "Despooking: Scary Moments." Know that all horses require both types of training.

If you are training up a very young horse, take special note: Sacking out and desensitizing will be an ongoing process for horses of all ages. (It never ends, not really.) However, the youngster in particular faces a steep learning curve and will rapidly transform from being terrified of (your hand, your waving shirt, a dropped feed bucket, etc.) to accepting the stimulus with a bored look. But don't be fooled by this with young horses (most specifically). Six months from now you'll still be dealing with a youngster who may accept your grooming nonchalantly - but uses logic at best sparingly so extra caution is always in order. Half a year later, it's still a "child." Trust it accordingly. Still, you'll be safer tomorrow in your handling - and can make a future ride safer - with the work you do here now. (The longest journey begins with the first step and all.)

Look at sacking out or "desensitizing" this way: When you ride, you cue your horse to move by clucking. If your horse moves and you keep clucking, you burn out that cue. You've taught the horse to ignore your request. Conversely, if you want your horse to stand still when you touch it with your hands or a saddle blanket, pretend you're trying to get it moving and keep applying "the cue" even after it's moving. Do it until you burn out "the cue." Rather than being work, it's almost fun when you see it this way.

When the horse moves on cue and you immediately halt your cue - or you back up an ignored cue with a good swift kick, you are "sensitizing." As you can see, sometimes this is good, sometimes it's bad. You can sensitize your horse to pressure on the reins, but you can also desensitize your horse to pressure on the reins. If you want him to become accustomed to something (dulled or desensitized), you continue the stimulus even after the horse is moving and continue for an extended period of time or until it stops moving; if you want him to become sensitized you remove the stimulus immediately when the horse moves. See the difference? It's important to understand that your horse is always learning and to be aware that you might be sharpening when you want dull.

To sack out your horse, tour your barn and surroundings, picking up buckets of objects, objects that range on the scariness scale from "probably not scary" to "guaranteed to scare." A hoof pick is probably not going to scare your horse, a crinkly-sounding feed bag probably will. Be sure to grab the obvious like a brush, feed bucket, saddle blanket, lariat, lunge whip, bell boots, halter, lead rope, bridle, etc. - but you may also want to get creative, placing a rock or two in a coffee can, tying two horseshoes together and so on.

You'll get your horse "over" each thing you pick up, so the more steps you put into this, the easier it'll be later when it comes time to put the halter on, or blanket, bathe or clip the horse. You'll literally need dozens of objects. Look over the stuff you've accumulated and mentally arrange them from least to most scary.

A note to the wise: At no point in the work that follows are you to push your horse into a true panic. There is a big difference between momentarily spooking your horse versus pushing it to "terrified." Apply common sense and back off any time the horse seems to be reaching panic status. You'll only be making things harder for both you and the horse. Note that youngsters don't have the mental (or physical) maturity of older horses that have grown more dull to the world in general, so in their cases use far, far less pressure. Youngsters can get scared and stay scared, obviously the opposite result from we're after. They're also more prone to reacting wildly and hurting themselves, so act accordingly.

Before using the objects you've collected, we'll begin by using a lunge whip. We'll use that lunge whip to safely gauge our horse's current attitude. Maybe our horse is feeling especially cantankerous today and if he is, we want to know that fact now rather than later. (Or, maybe we've never seen this horse before and don't know how to "read his mood.") Maybe it just seems tense. (Here are some clues: Are you seeing the "whites of his eyes"? Is he standing there, rigid, head and neck raised, back bowed, his feet planted? Tense!) In the interest of safety, grab your lunge whip (you know, the kind that's rigid for about four feet before attaching to several more feet of rope). If you've got one of those carrot sticks promoted by Pat Parelli or Clinton Anderson, you can use that, too. I like beginning with a lunge whip or carrot stick because it gives me the ability to test out the waters from a safe distance.

(If you have an older horse, don't skip the early, super-simple steps. You might find a hole in your horse's training that'll surprise you - and it also provides an objective point in your training that you can fall back to if you find later that you've pushed too hard.)

Station your horse with you in a pen (a round pen is best) and ask him to face you. The object of this game (here now with the lunge whip and later with your bucket of objects) is to bring the horse's emotions up a little, then lower them without causing him to move off. If he runs away, you lose points. Try less pressure next time, maybe a less-threatening angle or different body part. Your goal is to find a spot that gets a little rise out of him (a slightly raised head, a slight stiffening, etc.), then remove your stimulus and bring him back to calm, back to zero. Raising his blood pressure slightly and calming him back down wins you a point. (If he does move off, then you must keep applying the pressure (whatever you were wagging at him) methodically, desensitizing, burning your "cue," until he stops. Then reposition and start again.)

With the "rope part" of the lunge whip or carrot stick held up by your fingers to keep it from hanging loose, reach toward the horse and stroke his withers or the point of his shoulder once or twice then lower the lunge whip, smile broadly and say something nice. (You could begin with the horse's head, but I've found them to be more accepting of a touch to the withers or shoulder.) You may very well need to keep your contact to about a thousandth of a second, should the horse repeatedly move off. But that's okay, that's a start. Repeat this and sooner rather than later, your horse will begin to realize "Oh, that's all you wanted? No problem." He still won't trust you as far as he can throw you, but he'll soon let you dab his shoulders with the lunge whip if you simply stay with it.

Can't even get the whip to the horse? Back away and lightly smack the whip on the ground, snaking it about, toward the horse but back away before he can move off. If he does move away, keep moving the whip with the same intensity until the horse stops moving, then relax momentarily (to reward his stop), then start again. (Remember, if he moves off and you stop your twirling, you're sensitizing him to the whip as described earlier - which is the opposite of what we want to accomplish.) Build on this till you can raise the whip to his shoulder and finally touch him with it, however briefly. In other words, "start where you can." With more timid or younger horses, you may have only a second or two before he moves off. If this is the case, start with a millisecond build from there.

Practice this "advance/retreat" maneuver several billion times. Raise the whip, scratch the horse's back for 15 seconds, lower the whip and say something positive. One thing I like to do to break up the repetition is to occasionally simply turn my back on the horse and walk to the opposite side of the arena where I'll just hang out for thirty seconds or so. Horses are naturally curious and this can often pique their curiosity and cause them to become more "into" you. It mixes things up, can break up a good stalemate, and helps to keep the horse interested in you. (And it certainly reduces any threat he might feel.)

When the horse is thoroughly bored with his back being scratched, move your attentions to his neck. Then under his neck, down his front leg, over the length of his back, his belly and finally his back legs. Each time begin by rubbing something you've already worked on before moving to the new area. For instance, if he's okay with his shoulder being scratched, start there before trying his neck for the first time. This may initially take several sessions, but once they get the hang of this, they'll park out and just hang out, bored.

Ideally, you'll rub every spot for a count of 15, then lower your whip, take a few seconds breather, then repeat. You'll want to actively hunt the goosey spots (like between those back legs, under the tail, his ears, etc.) and concentrate on those until they no longer get a rise out of your horse. Trust me, you want to find those goosey spots and deal with them right now, here and today. Tell yourself that you'll get a hundred bucks for every goosey spot you can find and eradicate.

A word about ears: I'm a firm believer that the horses I'm called to fix that refuse to be bridled or blanketed or pick up their feet would never have become such large dangerous pills had their owners shown consistent yet kind discipline. A good old fashioned zero tolerance policy for crapola would have put an end to such poor behavior years before. With this in mind, I want you to promise yourself right now that you will work with your horse till those ears can be flipped, held, petted and otherwise manhandled without objections from your horse. Head shy horses are not only dangerous - they also label you as somebody who shouldn't own a horse. A green horn. A schlub. Frankly, I'm half-convinced that horses see the ability to avoid having their ears touched as a test: "Is this owner of mine a dufus or what?"

Being careful to stay clear of those kicking feet, set about testing out those ears. Some horses have been trained to this and simply won't care, others would rather die than have an ear bent forward. Dab as near to the ear as you can actually touch, rub and drop your whip as before. (Go easy, touch or stroke lightly; they're his ears after all.) If you can move one ear, great, flip it back and forth and check it off your list. To deal with an ear that doesn't want to be touched, the idea is "touch it so quickly" that the horse doesn't even have time to move off. Stay with it, keep calling him back if you need to, and gradually slow down the passes of your whip till he'll stand for more and more. If he gets irritated by this, tough beans. Do it some more. Who's paying the bills around here? Stick with this until you can flip his ears back and forth like light switches, until you can wrap the rope part of the whip around his ears lightly and until he stands there calmly as you do so. If he looks pissy, keep doing it till he becomes more accommodating. Later, when we begin using our hands to desensitize, make sure that you stick with it till you can squeeze (lightly) the base of his ears and also brush the tiny hairs within the ear back and forth - two tests he'll need to pass in the future, like when it comes time to bring out the clippers.

Moving on: Use the "rope part" of your whip to desensitize the horse's back legs. Bring the whip aside then smoothly toward the back legs, causing the rope to wrap around or between the legs. Give the rope a few tugs and do whatever wacky thing you can think of to get the horse accustomed to being touched there. Keep in mind that horses that kick back at objects that unexpectedly touch their feet are telling you that they'd do the same to your head if you fell off. Trust me, spend quality time desensitizing those back legs.

You might be tempted to try and hold the horse in place should he try to move off or pitch his head away. Don't do it. And don't chase after him. Chasing after the horse will serve as proof to him that you're not to be trusted. Trying to hold him in place will at best antagonize your horse, at worst it'll get you kicked. If he moves off bring him back with an inside turn or beckoning kiss. This can be tedious and will be sort of a pain for you, but in the end he will have learned the material better if he's not forced and comes to the conclusions on his own. Each time he takes his head away, relax and ask with a kiss to have him bring his head back to you. Get used to doing this; you'll have to "bring him back to you" several trillion times. (By the same token, if you get the feeling that the horse is just playing you, that he's not trying or bored with you, don't be afraid to clap your hands or do something else to wake him up, to keep him "sensitized." Send him around the pen a time or two at a jog to bring back his focus and create energy.)

It wouldn't be unheard of for the horse to signal that he's tired of you sometime during this exercise by trying to give you a good kick. Until recently, he's simply ignored your requests - but today you're pushing him so, until you gain his respect, be extra careful to stand clear (near the point of his shoulder, slightly off to the side) whenever practical. If he kicks (or even thinks about it as signaled by a threatening raise of a hind leg) scream your bloody head off and chase him away. Let him know immediately and in no uncertain terms that this is not acceptable behavior. (Same goes for nips.) He'll run around a bit, but you just need to bring him back to you and begin again.

Finally, you'll take up your "bucket of scary things" and use them to run through the same process you just did with the whip. Your hands will be the least scary objects, so begin by petting your horse where you can. Pet, retreat, relax, repeat, as described above. Be careful to always begin with an area where the horse stands relaxed (maybe his back, maybe his shoulders) and to move from there to the new spot (like his back legs). Remember to stand safely at the point of his shoulder when possible.

When the horse will stand there, his head dropped and neck relaxed, a soft and bored look in his eyes, you can move on to the next object. Maybe the brush or hoof pick to follow up your hands. Rub the hoof pick all over the horse till he's bored silly. The more objects you add in, the easier your "most scary object" will eventually be. When you work with objects that can be folded (towels, plastic bags, saddle pads), start with them folded and work like that till the horse stands relaxed - then open the object progressively until it no longer gets a rise out of him. (And practice opening the object as you approach him so that he gets the chance to see - and grow accustomed to - this magically growing object.) Don't forget to thoroughly desensitize those ears with each object before moving to the next.

Repeat this entire process until you can swab his entire body with your most scary object (like the heretofore terrifying plastic grocery bag). Also, make it a point to scratch or rub them in spots that they like to be scratched and rubbed, like the base of their necks, their withers and above their tails. I think this added effort goes along way to them seeing us as something positive rather than some person who always seems to mean work or scary things.

Despooking: Scary Moments

Here's how to teach your horse to contain himself (and thus, keep you safe) when something scary pops out of nowhere.

Note: While this exercise closely parallels the preceding chapter, "Despooking: Scary Things," there is a big difference at the heart of the training, (chiefly in how we "approach and retreat" with scary objects here versus rubbing the horse with the object). I've written it as "standalone" to eliminate confusion and for equestrians who find themselves with "one problem and not the other." Thus... while you'll find some of the steps redundant, I find any repetition in structure to be a necessary trade-off.

I've heard horse trainer and clinician Clinton Anderson say that if a horse were not born with a tail, but instead woke up with one tomorrow, he'd spend the day running away from the thing. As previously discussed, horses become desensitized to items that they spend their days with, things they come into contact with often: The hay rack, tack, or cat he sees everyday become no big deal. Cows scare "city" horses; they're no problem for ranch horses. You've actually seen this desensitizing in action on any horse that won't move forward, despite our kicks: He's learned that the kick doesn't hurt; he knows you'll soon tire - and frankly, he'd rather just stand there, thank you. Get on a green horse and give him a good kick and you'll likely end up on the ground. The old school horse has become so "used to it" that it (the kicks, the pleadings) have ceased to mean a darn thing.

Horses that don't trot off when asked need to be "re-sensitized" to our aids while spooky horses need to be "desensitized" (to our touch, to bug spray, to the saddle). But here's a very major point that you should bear in mind: You can spend your entire life desensitizing your horse to new and scary objects and never run out of material. Because of this, we treat items that might touch the horse or that he might come into contact with frequently (such as waving tarps, fly masks or saddle blankets) in a different fashion than the unknown situation that might arise on the trail or show grounds. Simply put, all horses require both sorts of training.

To arm ourselves against the "unknowns," we'll practice what John Lyons calls "Spook in Place." While we can never tell the horse to "not be scared," we can certainly teach him what to do with his feet when he does become spooked - and that's what this exercise is all about.

A word of caution: Exercises such as this, all by themselves, are not magic wands. If you're riding and look back to see your horse's hind legs above his rear end, it's too late to whip out this exercise or any other and hope it's going to save you. Sure, if your horse starts bucking you can (and should) disengage the hip and if he bolts you should do the same - but that's a last-ditch effort, a hail-Mary pass. Don't let it get to that point. Horses are living, breathing creatures with emotions and their own ideas of how they'd like to spend their time. Every moment you're riding you need to be engaging your horse, keeping it's mind on you. Build a firewall between yourself and danger by keeping your horse occupied, buy a little insurance by teaching exercises such as this ("Spook in Place") - but don't rely on one thing singularly. It's the totality of your work - and your good, common sense - that helps to keep you safe.

"Spook in Place" is one of many lessons your horse needs to be taught and here's what it's all about: You're out on the trail and something unexpected, perhaps a skunk, runs by. Maybe it's a motorcyclist, a plastic bag, a barking dog... it doesn't matter. As stated, we can't foresee every possible situation, and we can't expect to eradicate our horse's fear, so we need to teach our horse "how to deal." Your horse's ability to cope with "fright" in general must be progressively strengthened just as your muscles in the gym. We do this by raising and lowering the amount of "fear pressure" we exert under controlled circumstances and by, very purposefully, not touching the horse with any object we might use. We start by introducing him to .01 "pounds" of pressure, teaching him how to react at that point, and we build from there.

First, what you'll need to do is look around your house, yard or barn for "scary things." (Just as you did in the previous chapter.) That is to say, you need to go find 20 items that might scare your horse - but each to a different degree. The pen in your pocket will (most likely) not scare your horse as much as a blowing tarp and the cap on your head isn't as terrifying as a child's noise-making toy or a coffee can full of rocks. Find 20 objects (on all points of the horror spectrum), outfit your horse with protective boots, and head out to the paddock. (A round pen is best, but any small paddock will do. Use a long lead line attached to his halter and adapt the following if your only alternative is a very large area. Note: If you must use a line, only use it as an absolute last resort to keep your horse near if he tries to am-scray. Their understanding is far deeper when you use your body language to get your point across as opposed to relying on the crutch offered by a lead line.)

What we'll do must be seen as a game, a game that you want to win. As in "Despooking: Scary Things," your objective is keep the horse from moving; you lose a point any time he so much as takes a step. And, as before, you are to show the horse scary objects and get a rise out of him - but in such a manner that he doesn't move away from them. Remember, he takes a step, it costs you a point.

In your mind, take the items you've accumulated and place them in an order, from least scary to most scary. Number one would be a hoof pick, number twenty would be a chain saw. Pick up number one and stand on the opposite side of the pen from your horse with your back turned to him. Turn around, ask him to keep two eyes on you, and "reveal" your least scary object. Ideally, the horse will just stand there, staring. If he does anything more than prick up his ears, find an object that's not so scary and begin again. You'll turn, reveal the object and perhaps whisper "boo." Your horse will take notice, but most likely do nothing. You will then put the object down and walk over to your horse. Pet him and return to the opposite side.

Next, start adding intensity to your "boos" and movements. Say "boo" in a speaking voice, maybe throw in a wave. Watch the horse and if he just looks back, drop your object and calmly walk over to pet him. If he turns and walks off, ask for an inside turn, get his two eyes back on you and begin again. From here you will transition from a whisper to a speaking voice to a shout; you'll wave, clap, dance around. With each rendition, you will increase the intensity to a point where you get some small reaction from the horse. You're looking for him to prick his ears forward, snort or raise or lower his head. You want his emotions to rise a bit. Release the pressure when you get this reaction, drop any object you might be holding, calm yourself, and pet your horse. It's time to increase your intensity when the horse no longer reacts to an object.

Again, your goal is to keep the horse in one place, to not scare him so much that he takes off, but to get a little reaction out of him each time. But what to do if he scoots away? If he moves off just a few steps, you'll simply ask for an inside turn, bring the two eyes back onto you and start again. Be on the lookout, though, for the horse that moves off then pauses as if he's thinking "maybe I should stay." That's a very good sign. Our lesson is starting to sink in; he's thinking. When that horse returns to you make sure you praise profusely. If he takes off and makes it a quarter turn or more around the pen ask for an inside turn (a turn in toward you) and be careful to bring him back in the direction from which he took off. (That is, if he takes off to your right, don't allow him to return from the left following a run around the ring. Make him turn inside and come back from your right.) If he tears off at a million miles an hour, let him go, but push him through several rotations. Make him understand that dodging off is not the answer, in fact, it means more work. Dissuade this with a handful of laps around the pen. Be very careful to not allow your horse to get in the habit of simply running a lap, then coming back to you. That's not going to force change in his mind.

The idea is that we raise and lower the horse's emotions like a rubber band being pulled then released. Each time he looks at the object and keeps his feet in one place, he finds a release. With repetition, his reactions become less severe and we find that we can expose him to an object that just the day before terrified him.

When you can dance about, wave your arms and holler holding object number one - with little or no reaction from the horse - it 's time to up the ante, so' to speak. Pick up object two and repeat the process: Expose the object to the horse, increase the intensity in your voice or body language until you get a small reaction from your equine partner, then drop the pressure and pet your pet. Don't use an object once the horse is no longer reacting to it. The purpose of this is not to "deaden" him to a particular something, it's to condition his response.

Despooking: Scary Places

Does you horse turn into a basket case every single solitary time he gets near the same darn spot on the trail or seemingly innocent patch of arena dirt? Here's your fix.

Wanna get your horse over his fear of a particular spooky spot on the trail or in your arena so you can ride in those areas safely without having to divert like some pilot avoiding a storm? Does that blowing flag or herd of shape-shifting goats make every ride a maddening battle of wills? If so, then the first thing to do is to develop a training plan that has a beginning, middle and end: In the "beginning," you can't ride "over there." You ride around frustrated and you read stuff like this. In the "middle," you train and train and train. In the end, you reach your goal. Your goal is to ride safely WHERE YOU CANNOT TODAY. Remember: We don't start with our goals; we work toward them. Don't force your horse to carry you into dangerous territory this afternoon just because "you want to."

(People ignore this advice daily; it's one of the reasons we have helmets.)

If you want to ride "there" - but you know from experience that "there" freaks out your horse, then take the time necessary to build up to that. Avoid placing yourself and your horse in situations where you're just asking for trouble. Instead, ride where you feel yourself to be reasonably safe today, doing exercises designed to strengthen the control you have over your horse. Tomorrow, build on that.

Things can take a bad turn anywhere, sure - but riding where it's safe(r) today, investing the time it takes to build more control into your horse where you inherently have more control, (as opposed to dangerously forcing the issue), will not only keep you safer, but any added training you do will pay dividends later. Light a candle, don't curse the darkness, and you'll come out miles ahead.

Know right off that some horses (maybe yours, maybe not yours) are going to breeze through their training in a day, others weeks, others even longer. Given that, don't rush things - for your own safety's sake. What difference does it make if you get out past that scary garbage can today or next month? If you enjoy riding and spending time "hanging out" with your horse, then trading the "scary place" for exercises designed to gain control is still "quality time in the saddle." Win-win, as they say.

Develop your course of action: First, consider the place that causes your horse to "lose it," (where he bucks, rears, prances, bolts, etc.) Is it you riding past that chained dog? Next to the highway? The blowing tarp covering the hay? Next, ask yourself where you can ride where the horse would be completely calm. If riding next to the tarp causes bucking and is hence a "10" on our scale, then what constitutes a "1"? You will start at "1" and work progressively through all the numbers (read: "places") before finally reaching "10." (Think of the safe spot and come up with 10, 20 or even 100 "areas" between there and the hot zone.) If you feel his emotions welling up at any point, back off and add more steps to your plan, more "numbers." Maybe you need twenty or thirty steps in your plan, ten might be pushing too hard.

So, if your horse is calm 100 yards from the blowing tarp, you start there, doing any simple exercise you've ever learned with concentration and precision. Work to make something, anything, better. Maybe you work to place his right front foot more precisely on "x," maybe you work to get a quicker backup, maybe you refine the arc in his neck. When the horse will stay focused on you, ride momentarily into the "gray zone" adjacent to your safety zone and then back again. A moment later, repeat your sneak and, if he stays calm, inch over. Claim this new space and continue your training. Train until he's calm, stray momentarily "into the gray," then back, inch over if "he's cool with it," repeat. Maybe you can progress today every few minutes or so, maybe progress takes days or months. Regardless, the object is to gradually build up your control through improved performance. The horse never actually forgets the scary object exists, he just becomes progressively better trained to following requests.

Note: If your horse is "fine" at home but spooks in the show arena, making "inching closer" impractical or impossible, see the follow-up chapter, "Despooking: Scary 'Away' Places," which expressly deals with this situation.

If your horse can't seem to get past a certain point, it means you have to break your training into yet more steps; you're rushing things.

There's theory to this training and it goes like this: Years ago John Lyons used to tell of a boy and a girl who begin dating. The girl is appalled at the big green chair the boy sits in daily to watch his football games: It's ratty and garish. He, however, loves it. It's comfortable and broken in. The girl, however, on this first date, he can take or leave. She understand this weakness and willingly overlooks it - for now. The two hit it off and time passes; the girl is careful to never mention the green chair. They are married and one day the new husband returns to find his chair not in the center of the room, but over in the corner. She calms him, saying something like "Moving the chair puts you closer to the fridge, honey." Wow! How does he argue with that? That makes terrific sense and he only wishes he'd thought of it himself. Days turn into months and every so often, he returns to find his chair "just that much closer" to the garage door. Finally, one day he comes home to find it... egad, actually in the garage. He mentions this to his wife who says something like "But, honey, I haven't even SEEN you sit in that chair in months, what with you being so busy running to Lowe's, Home Depot and whatnot...."

It took her years, but she's rid of the chair. And never once did she lose her patience, did he get mad or did they fight about it. Had she turned up her nose on the first date and said the chair's gotta go, she might have gotten dumped (like you in the saddle) and she knew that.

The point is: Don't move into your horse's house and go trying to rearrange the furniture on day one. Every horse has got a green chair; pitch it without a thought and he just might pitch you. With any relationship, you've got to ease in there. Ask for gradual change.

That's today's big concept. Don't move your horse's green chair out to the garage on day one. If the row of garbage cans scares the devil out of him - but he's okay skirting them by 40 feet, begin looking for ways to move the chair one inch at a time. That means breaking up your training as I described above, one step at a time. It means today you practice your disengagements 40 feet from the cans and move to 39 when he's relaxed. Tomorrow you practice at 39 then 38. Maybe you'll move closer today, maybe tomorrow, maybe next week. Maybe you'll move ten feet closer each time, maybe a hundred. Your horse will tell you clearly if he becomes agitated; jiggy horses mean you're moving too quickly.

Despooking: Scary 'Away' Places

When your horse only turns into a freakzoid when you've trailered to a distant location - like a show - here's what to do.

We address the horse that acts a fool only in the arena or "away from home" with speed control exercises. Why? Because if we're dealing with horses that are fine at home - but nutso in the arena, then at first blush, it seems as if we only have two choices: Work with the horse in a situation when he's calm and there's "nothing to fix" (the home stable) or when he's freaked and schooling is difficult at best (during a show, or at the side of a cliff as his buddies move away). One choice doesn't give us much to work with, the other is just plain unsafe or impractical. Speed control gives us a method to reproduce these emotional moments under more controlled situations so that we can deal with the issue methodically, objectively, and on our terms.

Any time we add speed, we up the horse's emotion level, right? We'll use that to our advantage here to create a situation that mimics the anxiety the horse feels in the show arena or when separated from his buddies on the trail. It's not comfortable for the horse to spend his time being scared any more than it is for you to feel the same way, perhaps more so, him being a prey animal and all. Get him agitated and there's nothing he'd love more than to not be. Believe it or not, he doesn't want to stay excited - he wants to munch grass and snooze. It's just that some horses have learned that acting like a jerk scares you off - and that's the quickest route he's found back to the barn.

Both situations described above make one thing clear: Speed control gives us mind control. We'll strengthen his "emotion muscle" by continually working and flexing that brain of his. Over and over we will amp him up, then shut him back down. Each time we do so, we build a little more strength in him emotionally, a little more ability in his mind to deal with more stressful situations.

When we continually raise his emotions - just barely so that we retain control - by asking for increased speed, then shut him back down again (slow down to walk, pet, relax) it won't take him long to figure out that simply staying calm is a whole lot easier. The trick is to do each increase in small increments.

Here are two exercises to use:

One way to teach your horse to travel at a myriad of speeds within a specific gait, is to move up in your gears and then ease back down over and over. Ease up, then cut your speed ("throttle back") and repeat. While doing so, remember that adding speed adds emotion (which is why we're doing this), and that probably means increased stiffness through his body. Be on the lookout for this and employ a zero tolerance policy toward any sort of resistance in the form of bracing, stiff muscles, lurching, etc. That is, if your horse becomes stiff as you increase speed, fix it before preceding. Cancel your plans to work on speed control per se and instead work on softening. (Do serpentines: Pick up a single rein as he turns, hold the rein till his neck relaxes or drops, walk forward, repeat the other way - again and again with an eye toward calming your horse.)

In a safe environment, get on your horse and walk off. Don't pull back on the reins, but really sit down in the seat and concentrate on slowing him down. Your "dead weight" may naturally slow him down - or not. Either way, ask yourself how many miles an hour you're traveling and remember it. Now, lean forward a bit, "ride faster" with your seat, move your arms (and thus the reins) forward, kiss, cluck like a chicken, whatever it takes to move your horse faster. You want to push your horse up as fast as it'll travel in a walk. If it breaks into a trot, that's okay, just ease it back down. Now, remember that fastest speed you were just given. Let's say the slow speed you clocked was three, the faster speed six. Your horse is capable of traveling in that range of speed (3-6) today. You'll set it as your goal to broaden that range.

Is this you? You think your horse is about to slow down so you give him a good kick? That makes sense to you - but the horse figures he got kicked for no good reason. You'll burn out your "move faster" cue quick that way. I need you to start thinking and riding differently.

Instead, continue this exercise by walking your horse forward and asking it to speed up; demand a "noticeable change of leg speed." If your horse was traveling at 4 mph, ask for faster and make sure he does just that. It's not a maybe it's a definitely. If he doesn't speed up, kick until he does. If he breaks into the next higher gait, ease him back down and keep trying.

If your horse begins to slow down on his own when you travel 30 feet at the increased speed, then ask him to slow down the next time at 28 feet. It's key that you ask for the slow down - it's not supposed to be his idea. Remember, you don't want to be in the habit of kicking him when you "think" he's going to slow down so you've got to make the first move. Ask him to slow a moment before you think he was going to slow down anyway. You'll concentrate on building the range your horse first gave you; if it was 7 and 10, see if you can't build that out in small increments to 5 and 14, 2 and 16, etc.

You'll find that you have a broader range as you continue to practice - and you're horse will also begin to stay at a particular speed on his own for increasingly longer periods of time. Practice this at a walk until you've increased the range dramatically and things feel fluid. Next, a trot and finally a lope when you feel safe doing so.

The next exercise is one of my favorites because it's an idiot-proof way to easily raise and lower, raise and lower, a horse's emotions under controlled situations. And, not only does it instill speed control, but horses just learning to canter, buckers and those who "have a cow" when asked to lope will also benefit.

This exercise is usually practiced from a trot into a canter - but there's no reason why you can't practice first going from a walk into a trot if your horse is overly agitated or you just need to find a rhythm. Here's what you'll do:

Pick up a trot. Trot forward perhaps thirty feet as you plan what you're going to do. Use that time to slowly and methodically ask your horse to canter. Move into the canter for exactly four strides, then shut your horse back down to the trot. Bear in mind that your body will actually have to move faster as the horse slows into the trot due to the change of cadence. Be prepared to actually speed up your seat as he slows down. Doing so will make you a better rider and keep you from interfering with cues you're giving.

You'll continue trotting, using the next 30 or 40 feet to prepare. Ask for the lope (or "canter" if your saddle has no horn), and shut the horse back down immediately after the fourth stride. Do your level best to make it exactly four strides because the objectivity will help prove to you whether you have control or not.

What you'll find with horses that typically become agitated when asked to lope is that after 10, 20, or 30 minutes of this speed up, slow down business, they'll begin to relax. Why? Because they see the rhythm, realize it's a simple request and that it's no big deal. We're just asking them to lope a few strides, not forcing a new gait down their throats with no end in sight. Horses who are new to loping don't know how to balance themselves and the rider. They feel like they're going to tip over and speed up to compensate, in effect using centrifugal force to keep from falling over. It takes time for them to learn balance and build the necessary muscle. Until then catering can be a frightening thing best eased into.

Repetition shows them that a little speed and a different gait is nothing to be scared of. By practicing just four strides before shutting down then immediately repeating, we're getting in a lot of little practices fast.

Don't forget, use your "trotting time" to prepare and relax. Get your four strides at a canter, shut the horse down to a trot. Trot, canter, shut 'er down.

Here's why the owner of a jittery horse needs to practice speed control: Not long ago I was conducting a clinic in some far-off state. I had the group practicing the same exercise just described. One of the riders called me over and said "This exercise might be something these other riders need, but not me. I'm not doing it." I asked her why she was in the clinic; what was she wanting to accomplish. She replied that she spent quite a bit of time on the trail and that barking dogs caused her horse to buck. She wanted to fix just that. Only that. I asked her if her horse was capable of doing the exercise the others were doing; could it trot, canter four strides calmly and shut back down without an issue? She admitted that her horse did become a "tad bit unhinged" during the cantering part. To this I replied "You came here because your horse bucks at the sight of a barking dog. So let's imagine that that dog applies 100 pounds of emotional scary pressure to your horse and your horse just can't take it. You've also said that your horse isn't capable of moving smoothly through this exercise which applies maybe 6 pounds of pressure. How do you expect your horse to ever withstand 100 pounds if you haven't taken the time to get him past six?" She thought about it, smiled and said "Now that makes sense. I'll do it."

Which drops us off nicely at today's big concept: If your horse freaks at 100 pounds of pressure (the show pen, barking dogs, rushing traffic, gunshots), take the time to use the things you've learned here to build him up from 2 pounds to 100 plus.

Say Good-Bye to Mr. Jiggy

Here we'll learn to relax and slow a high horse with a method so simple that it only has one step.

This is a little trick with huge results. It puts the kibosh on jiggy prancing - and it softens even the toughest-mouthed horses along the way.

What if you came out to train your horse and it was jigging, just prancing all over the place? Every time you touch the reins the head shoots up and you've got a big fight on your hands?

Your horse does that for one or both of two reasons: He's doing it because it's a bad habit he's learned and/or because he's scared and it's all part of his "flight or fight" programming. Nature has programmed him to head for the hills the instant he feels danger -- and pulling on a rope tied to his head with all our might is probably a pretty clear sign to the untrained horse that something's amiss, so he struggles. And we react by fighting to keep him contained. And his flight turns into our fight.

Where to begin? Every time you touch those reins it just seems to escalate...

The simple tip that follows opens a back door, a way to sneak in and begin training the horse without him realizing that you've gotten one over on him. Use it anytime you need a starting point to begin working with a flighty horse. Will it turn a wild beast into a kid's horse in twenty minutes? Duh, of course not. But it's a great way to start getting your horse to listen to you.

WHAT YOU'LL DO: Today when you ride, pick up a trot to the right and try the following:

STEP 1) pick up your right rein and find the angle and amount of pressure it takes to move the horse's butt one step to the left BUT KEEP MOVING FORWARD then release the rein.

Relax your reins, compose your thoughts for at least four strides, keep moving on your circle and repeat this sequence for twenty minutes.

STEP 2) There is no Step Two. How simple is that? You've calmed an agitated horse and it took one brain cell to do it. You can think about anything or nothing while your do this. As long as you simply feel for, and release on, his hip stepping over, it's idiot proof.

(Yes, you can do this at a walk, but the simple fact for most exercises is this: at a walk you learn the maneuver - at a trot the horse learns. Both gaits have their place.)

THREE WAYS TO SCREW THIS UP:

If you allow the horse to stop moving at any point, you'll gain little from this exercise. You'll actually be teaching it to resist bit pressure and your cues... so, don't. Focus on keeping your horse moving fluidly every second until you are finished with your practice. The whole point is to get the horse to give (to bit pressure and hence "our will") while moving out and forward. Keep reading for suggestions.

Make sure that you relax the reins in between repetitions. (When you're riding in neutral, I'd expect to see an actual bow in that rein, a real "droop.") Otherwise the horse thinks it's a twenty minute exercise. More importantly, he won't be getting a break from your pressure so he won't calm down.

If you get bored and start meandering around and fail to practice this for a good solid 20 minutes, you can kiss your results good-bye. Stay on your circle. Make it a bigger or smaller circle, but stay on it and keep moving. There is no dawdling in horse training.

Keep in mind when doing any new exercise is that you need to keep your hands moving smoothly and slowly. Take it at a walk when you first begin; hold off on applying speed until both you and your horse understand the correct steps.

WHAT TO DO IF the horse just won't move his darn hip: First try changing the way you're using your hands. Try more pressure. Try less pressure. Try different angles, maybe faster, maybe slower. (Hint: Asking for increased speed will help, nine out of ten times.)

If that doesn't work, walk along a fence, apply pressure to the inside rein (nearest the fence) and release that pressure after the horse moves his hip (to the right if the fence is on the left). Don't complete the turn. Instead, drop the direct rein (the left) as soon as you feel him move that hip and get him going back the original direction right away, with zero hesitation preferably. Travel several beats, then repeat. He'll soon make the connection that you picking up that inside rein (left in our example) means "move his hip" (to the right). Of course, you'll repeat going both directions and can move away from the fence when he understands your cue.

If you don't feel safe and need an interim step or maybe you feel like you're trying to bend a two thousand pound rock and he's out-muscling you, then let's make it simpler for both of you. Remember, the objective is to teach the horse to "give to pressure" right? ("Give to pressure" means to not pull away from the bit, but rather to relax his muscles and to bend smoothly, fluidly.) So, walk off, meandering in any direction and simply pick up the rein and ask him to soften his neck muscles or drop his head as he takes a step. The direction doesn't matter -- but see if you can't keep the movement fluid, especially when you pick up the reins and apply pressure. Then let go, praise, repeat. When you can get a bit of softness going in any direction, try "softening on the turn," then work your way to getting the hip to move. It's important, though, that much more often than not, you're releasing as the horse is turning. Why? Because the horse needs to associate the reins with a change of direction.

If he stops, ease up on your rein pressure and get him going, (but do keep some pressure on the rein so he knows you're still looking for something) then ask again for a little softness. If he backs up, same thing. Ease up on your pressure, get him going forward, then ask for a bit of softness before releasing fully.

HOW TO MAKE THIS EASY ON YOURSELF: If you get greedy and ask the hip to move more than a step off the track it's on, it'll get harder and harder to keep the average horse moving. (Or, if your horse is completely wired, it'll just turn into a fight.) We just want a smaaaaaall movement here. Try to get that hip to move over almost without the horse realizing he's done it. Think of it this way as you ride: If after ten minutes it's getting harder instead of easier and you just want to quit and sell the horse, then it's one of two things: You're asking for too much hip movement - OR your horse is entirely too stiff through his neck. If "too stiff" is the answer, soften just the neck as outlined in the previous paragraph, concentrating on moving forward at all costs, then come back to the tail, so' to speak. What you've been doing is simply asking for too much - as evidenced by the fact that the horse resists moving forward.

NOTE: You can certainly do this in a serpentine pattern, but you'll keep it simple and have better luck keeping to one direction.

Pay particular attention to the feeling you get when the horse moves its hips. Really feel for it and memorize the sensation. You're going to need to recognize that movement to get more advanced maneuvers like flying lead changes.

WHAT THIS WILL ACCOMPLISH: This slows the horse in the same way a boat would be slowed (from moving forward) if you were to pick up the rear end and move it slightly to the right. For just a moment all that power stops driving forward and just sorta dissipates. It makes a good way to calm or slow the high-strung horse because when you simply pick up the rein till he takes a step over and release, your horse keeps moving forward and never feels trapped. There's no need to fight because you're not cutting off his flight.

It has the positive effect of causing your horse to relax his neck and drop his high head. It accomplishes this because the horse learns that when you pick up the reins, you're not looking to get into a wrestling match - you just want him to move his hips. (In fact, take note: Because a lowered head is a natural by-product of this exercise, this is an excellent thing to do even with the calm horse, when you simply want to teach a horse to lower his head.)

Finally, it also has the bonus of teaching your horse to cope properly with bit pressure. Remember, any time you pick up the reins, you're asking (or causing) your horse to slow down because his natural inclination will be to resist the bit. Teach the horse to soften while continuing to move out fluidly and you'll be well on your way to more advanced maneuvers that require collection like stops, turns, rollbacks, lead departures and changes, etcetera.

How to Slow Down Your Too-Fast Horse

If you have problems with your horse getting "higher and higher" -- or need a way to slow a fast one down -- then this is for you.

I want you to remember this simple thought: When you want to teach your horse to slow down, a simple key is to find a moment when that horse is traveling on a loose rein — and build on it. (You should underline that, then tattoo it on your wrist; it's that important.)

If you are constantly riding your horse, tugging on the reins to get him to slow down, then what you're really doing is teaching the horse two things: 1) Pressure from your legs is not the cue to speed up and 2) A loose rein is the cue to speed up.

Huh? How can that be?

See, it's the opposite of what you might think. Look at it from your horse's perspective: "When I'm slowing down, she pulls on my mouth. She doesn't pull on my mouth until I speed up. Aha! If I want a release, I gotta speed up."

Couple that thought with your horse's "fight or flight" instinct ("I'm gonna run or buck if I can't get away") — and you've built a rocket to ride.

The solution is this: First tell yourself the obvious: "I'll never find any moments of 'traveling on a loose rein' if I don't ever let go of the reins." Second, even if you feel that your horse is constantly pulling and tugging on the reins like a struggling pack of Alaskan huskies, look for those brief moments when your horse isn't pulling "as hard" on you and build on that. Better still, try to fabricate those moments by making what's correct the easy thing for him to do, and what's wrong the hard thing to do.

When you're on the trail and your horse begins moving his feet too fast or dances about, ask him to do some small task that he's already good at, something simple like "move your shoulder to the right one step" (then pause and repeat, pause and repeat) or "bring your hip over to the left a step," etc. Put him to work, doing something easy, objective and repetitious for several minutes, feeling all the while for a brief moment when you release the rein AND YOU CAN FEEL THE HORSE WANTING TO SLOW for any reason.

* If you're not simply "joy riding" when your horse acts up, if you're already training, then give him more to do, something more complicated. Maybe "move your hips to the right" becomes "move your hips to the right, then drop your head, then soften your neck, then move your shoulder, then..." etc. Don't up your own intensity level, just put more on his plate.

Then, in that fractional moment when you feel him slow, you have two options:

1) Ride slower, move slower, see how long the "moment" lasts — and QUIT the extra exercise. Go back to your quiet trail ride. The horse thinks "Funny, I slowed down and suddenly I didn't have to work so

hard." When the horse speeds up again (perhaps one second later, maybe two minutes later) then go back to the exercise (rather intensely) and wait for him to signal that he'd like to move slowly. Then you quit again. The horse comes to associate hard work with shenanigans and will start to think twice before acting up.

Or, try:

2) Ride slower, move slower, see how long the "moment" lasts — and CONTINUE the exercise, feeling patiently for that moment when he again slows up, your cue to react in kind. Beyond teaching your horse to calm, this second option will go further toward training your horse in other aspects: He'll turn to the right sharper, stay softer, etc. And, while sharpening his performance, you will have captured his attention and made it easier to get it the next time.

Both options work. Experiment to see which is right for you, when and where.

The key in all of the exercises is this: You've got to look for every opportunity to relax those reins. Quit pulling. Horses aren't nags, neither should you be.

You may have a horse that wants to take off at a dead run if you give him back any amount of rein. If that's the case, then try your level best to ride with the least amount of pressure you can and each time the horse begins to speed up, take a single rein and turn his tail "the way you don't want to go." Example: Your horse speeds up, you take the left rein and apply the pressure it takes to get the left shoulder to stop and the hip to move several steps to the right.

Or, a more subtle move: Try picking up a single rein and ask the hip to move but one step off the track he's on. Keep moving and do this over and over. Remember, every horse and rider combination is different. What works at some particular moment or situation, may not work in another, so don't get locked into doing certain steps in a certain way -- experiment to see what produces results and adapt.

Here's the perfect exercise to plug into this sort of situation:

1) Pick up a trot, then your left rein

2) Ask your horse to turn to the left by applying pressure

3) Keep applying pressure as your horse turns left and hold

4) Let go when the horse releases his pull on the rein or drops his head

5) Trot straight forward two steps, pick up your right rein

6) Repeat, creating a serpentine pattern

This is an exercise you should practice everyday (forever) when you first get on your horse. It's also a good "cool down" to bring your horse's emotions down any time they've risen. Just remember our perennial rule: The longer you hang onto the rein, the less you should release on.

If your horse develops a rubber neck (simply throws his head way over to the left by your boot and leaves it there) resist the temptation to pull his head back with the opposite rein. Instead keep hold of the rein, but change your "angle of attack" until you feel his hind end/hips step over to the side, then release. In effect you'll be saying "Nice try, but it's your choice, either simply turn and soften your head -- or move your big ol' fat butt." It's more work to move their hind end, so they'll quickly begin opting for the easier route, turning fluidly from the front.

Be careful to stay focused and feel for the horse softening - sometimes we start pulling so hard we don't realize that the horse couldn't relax even if he wanted to.

Remember: To work on a horse's speed, start by build on those moments when you're traveling on a lose rein; get control of the rear end (where the power comes from, practice lots of disengagements), and follow-up by working the front end (like the exercise I just described to get lightness).

In the end, by practicing this material, (and by "thinking differently" as outlined) you will have taught your horse to regulate his speed — and you would have done so safely, without a fight. Along the way you would have improved his performance, creating a horse that is safer to ride, picks up his leads more reliably, trots more comfortably, moves more smoothly and is a pleasure to ride.

Calm Down Now

Nature placed an On/Off switch onto each horse. This exercise gives you the "flip switch."

This is something you can use to calm your horse when you're out riding and he seems to be "an accident looking for a place to happen." You can also use it to aid in "framing up" your horse in everyday training or to reprimand him when he tries to nip another, nearby, horse.

In a nutshell, you will teach the horse to drop its head below its withers because doing so has a great calming effect. (Note: But you gotta stay proactive; read on.) When practiced to perfection, you should be able to pick up your reins gingerly with two fingers (like holding a stinky sock) to a height of about two inches - and the horse will drop his head like a rock in a pond.

The exercise is really very simple and can be accomplished quickly with most horses in under half an hour, sometimes in minutes: Sitting on your horse with it just standing there, take up the reins evenly and smoothly with both hands. Lay your legs against the horse and then drop them back away (though do maintain rein pressure). Picking up the reins and dropping your legs against his sides are pre-cues that say "Hey, I'm gonna be needing something outta you in just a sec." (A great habit to get in the habit of if you want to develop collection later.) If you were to lay a wet towel over your arm, that's about the amount of pressure you want to briefly apply against the horse's sides - which is not much.

Your legs will quickly drop away from the horse's sides but you'll continue applying even pressure with both reins, waiting. Very important: Keep even pressure throughout this exercise, moving your arms to follow his head if necessary.

You'll apply even skyward pressure on the reins until you feel the horse begin to pull his head down toward the ground. Why would he? Beyond the fact that it takes energy out of your horse to hold his head up, he'll do it because you're pulling up and like a teenage human, he resists anything that wasn't his idea. The instant the horse pulls down, even one bazillionth of a pound's worth, you release. This is one rare case where we're teaching the horse to pull against the reins. He'll gladly oblige because he just wants your fingers out of his mouth.

You'll want to gradually release, rather than "all at once." Don't drop the reins, but rather take one or two seconds to follow his release. The horse thinks he's getting away with something - but it's a something we wanted the whole time.

After repetition - and in a matter of moments - your horse will be dropping his head almost to the ground. We know, then, that he clearly understands to drop his head, so it's time to use less and less pressure. You want to get to the point where you can simply raise the reins with your thumb and forefinger and his head will drop. It becomes comical at this point because your horse will look as though he KNOWS he's pulling one over on you. Simply try a little less pressure with each request, amping your pressure only if necessary.

Note that your objective is to teach the horse that picking up the reins means "drop your head" as opposed to "drop your head this much" or "drop your head to here." That means that if you pick up the reins and he raises his head waaaaay up in the air, then you release when his head drops from the highest point reached since you picked up the reins. (Not lower than when you first picked up the reins.) Consequently, there may be times when you must release with his head up in the air. That's okay. Don't think "The head has to be at x-feet" think "The head just has to drop."

If the horse begins to back up you can either pull his hips around to stop him or, even easier, shrug it off and let him back up. If you choose to stop him by moving his hips around, immediately resume the even pressure and keep a calm attitude as you wait for the head to lower. If he backs, remember that he'll have to stop sooner or later; just go for the ride. Pretend you're standing still and release when he drops his head. About half the horses will back at first - but they all learn to stop doing so rather quickly - so don't be put off by it. Think about it: Backing takes energy, dropping their heads is easy. If the horse begins to walk forward, same answer, maintain your focus and release only when the head sinks however slightly.

It helps for you, the rider, to build muscle memory, because an erratic, halting lesson will only confuse the horse. Here, then, is the sequence to lock in: Pick up both reins and apply even pressure (about 3 pounds); lay your legs against the horse's sides lightly and immediately drop them back away; wait for the horse to pull down however slightly and release, allowing your hands to be briefly pulled down. Repeat. Your horse will get the idea quickly and in a few minutes he'll start dropping in feet not inches.

When your horse will immediately drop his head at a stand still, the natural progression is to then practice to perfection the entire sequence at a walk, then trot and finally at a lope. Remember that each time you add speed you also add emotion which seems to cause a memory lapse. Your horse will seemingly forget everything at a trot that he learned at a walk and so on. Expect this phenomena, stay patient, and work your way up through the gaits.

Caveat: This exercise teaches the horse to place its head at a particular position based on your release. What often occurs when folks begin practicing is that the horse will try to avoid any bit pressure by dropping his head "too low" or by pulling away and down. That's a typical reaction and easily fixed. Sometimes it happens days later when you're working on another exercise. Whenever it happens, you should simply begin holding the rein till the head gets into proper position and his pull softens, then release. The idea here is that the horse will learn that when you release the pressure, that's where he's to hold his head. This training concept holds true whether the head is too high or too low.

Gaited horse owners, take note. If you practice this exercise and find the horse dropping his head too low you have not "broken your horse." As above, you will simply apply pressure and time, waiting till the horse puts his head at the correct level, (even if that's higher rather than lower) then release. It's natural and typical for horses to sort of have fun at our expense through this exercise once they've learned it. Corrections are part of the process. (And don't forget, "long and low" is a similar exercise used to limber up gaited horses and it's been around forever.)

If the horse pulls "rudely," that's okay when first beginning to give him the idea to put his head down. But if that morphs into continued rudeness (he drops it too far, too often, or does it to avoid the bit) or he rubber bands his head, (snapping it up or down) then begin hanging on for a moment longer till you get "politeness."

What about the horse that just sits there? If you get the feeling you could be there for hours, apply a bit more pressure, perhaps at a different angle. (A few pounds more, not tons more.) If that doesn't work, simply begin drumming your legs against his sides, very lightly and rhythmically. (The rhythm is important.) If still no change, bump a little harder with the legs. (Having to apply extra motivation as outlined is exceedingly common and the odds are more than 50-50 you'll have to do this to some extent. Be ready.)

If your horse isn't progressing through this exercise, if it seemingly stalls out, then either apply more motivation (that means slightly more intense rhythmic bumps from your legs) or begin looking for smaller changes out of your horse. Take note, however: The initial movement from your horse will be slight, not dramatic. Get the horse to pull or drop just a little at first, maybe his head just lowers a hair. Build on that.

Warning: If you believe your horse might rear - or if you feel him growing "lighter on the front end, then back off on your pressure, (because, no matter what you might think, your horse is telling you that you're pulling too hard). Change your focus from "drop your head" to "move forward and soften your neck to one side." Get him moving forward (very, very important) and spend some time simply picking up the rein (lightly) until he softens the muscle in his neck on that same side. Drop the rein then and take a few more steps, pet, and ask him to soften again. Do this at a walk, then trot and do it on both sides, working to eradicate the stiffness entirely. Rearing is monstrously dangerous, so stay thinking here and step aside from any other work to deal with it immediately and for however long it takes.

Frequently Asked Question: "How does the horse know to drop his head to his knees while I'm standing here and then to only drop it x-amount later when we're riding?" Answer: With practice, a combination of factors will tell the horse what you're looking for: 1) The situation - the horse knows you typically ask for such-and-such while hanging out with your friends and something entirely different when rounding a barrel. (If you doubt this, then why does your horse know to run from the bridle in your hand but toward the feed bucket in your hand? Or to meet you at the gate at feeding time but to run away when you remove the halter? Or where the exit to the arena is or that you always stop loping at Frank's driveway?) 2) As stated, it's your release. Practicing this material gives you the ability to put the horse's head at any elevation simply based on when you release the reins. 3) Your body position. When you simply concentrate on something, you make small changes in the way you carry your body. Your horse reads this. Whether you're standing or being carried, your horse has nature's gift of reading body language innately.

Tip: As you release the reins, this will go much quicker if you release as if "reverse milking a cow." I'll explain: Put your hand out, making a fist. Now, one finger at a time, open your hand, starting with your pinky and working up toward your index finger. So, as the horse tugs on the reins, you will allow them to be pulled, you'll slightly drop your hands and arms to follow the motion - and finally you'll open your fist, one finger at a time, pinky finger then ring finger then bird finger then, lastly, index finger and thumb. (When you and the horse have learned this exercise, you can dispense with the theatrics and simplify your movements - but the exaggerated actions will help you communicate to your horse and find a rhythm in the beginning.) This seemingly bizarre tip will cause you to find the timing you need to hurry this particular exercise along.

Take heed...

The "Calm Down Cue" as described here is not a magic cure that calms your horse when he's three feet off the ground. It does not provide instant relief once things have gotten out of hand. For it to work, you must be proactive.

Here's an example - and it happened to me: Years ago I was riding one of my own horses; we'd just had a terrific session and this green horse had been pretty good. To cool out we took a casual walk around the equestrian center. She caught something out of the corner of her eye and in an instant she shot out from underneath me. In one trillionth of a second she was four feet to the left and I was hanging in the air like some cartoon character holding up a "Help" sign. I've never fallen straight down before or since; usually you get thrown to the left or the right. This happened so fast, however, that I dropped like a freight elevator.

Now, where exactly, during that one bazillionth of a second did I have time to do the "The Calm Down Cue"? I didn't have time to think the words, let alone do it.

I should have been doing the Calm Down Cue the entire time we were walking because I knew this horse's history of shenanigan-pulling. The horse had told me when she was jiggy in the preceding days that she couldn't yet be trusted. It's my bad, as they say. I should have never let my guard down.

What I learned that day was the importance of being a proactive rider. When you're riding any horse that isn't dead broke, you've got to keep making requests to keep that horse focused on you. When the horse spooks and you react, you are, by definition, a reactive rider. If you wouldn't bet your collar bone on the performance of your horse, then you are duty bound to keep that horse occupied at all times. That doesn't mean an intense workout at all times - that means keep making requests to keep the horse focused: drop the head, move the shoulder, soften the neck, etc. Had I been doing these things that day, the horse would have had it's mind on me, not the spooky object. Had it still seen the scary monster, I would have been in a better position (both physically and mentally) to deflect it's movements with a disengagement before the full-out eruption, not after.

Section II: Keeping Your Horse On the Straight and Narrow

What you do today determines the horse you'll ride tomorrow.

Perfect the First Time

If you're guilty of being a bit heavy-handed (as evidenced by a stiff-as-a-statue horse) here's a Top Five Horse Training Concept that will soften your horse fast.

Every single time you ask your horse to do something put the thought in your head that your horse will do it perfectly. That goes for handling him on the ground, riding him in the arena, bathing him, every interaction.

Huh? What if it's the first time I've ever asked this horse to do a flying lead change or to back up or to neck rein? Logic tells me there ain't no way.

First, as logic will also tell you, your horse was born knowing how to do all those things, you just have to figure out a way to tell him what you want. After all, if your horse could read English - and you held a sign up in front of his nose that said "put your left foot on the red leaf" - he'd do it nine out of ten times. The other one time would require some motivation, perhaps another sign that says "...and I'll keep showing you signs till you do it - and I got all day." The beauty is, those nine out of ten times? He'll move gracefully because he's not being pulled into position, he's simply "doing it."

The reason that you need to begin every exchange thinking "I know you will do this perfectly" is simple: Your brain will then cause your hands and body to ask the horse politely the first time - and then, should your horse not respond correctly (or at all), you can apply some motivation to help him find the answer. That is, you'd apply more rein pressure, try a different angle, etc. When you think different, you are different and so simply changing your thoughts will make a big difference very quickly.

Once I began teaching this simple concept in my clinics, it made a dramatic difference immediately. What I would first see were people who were thinking "Horse, you're not going to do this; I'm going to have to force you to do this." And then they'd yank. Again and again and again. What works exponentially better is to start with: "My horse stops on a dime every time; he's the best" (yes, even when the last four hundred times he didn't), then ask your horse to stop. If and when he blows through that stop, I want you to literally act shocked. Say out loud "I can't believe you just did that. I must not have spoken clearly enough." Then find the pressures or angle it takes to get a response.

Your hands and your release are everything. Any little trick you can learn to work more in concert with your horse will have a huge and positive impact. Make an effort to watch a rider (either in person, at a clinic, or on video) that you really respect. Especially watch the trainer's hands. Make note of when he releases and guesstimate the pressure he's using to get things done. Tell yourself "If he can do it, I can do it."

6 Easy Ways to Improve Your Training

Six horse training tips, each designed to simplify your training and make big changes fast

Sometimes the best way to improve our riding isn't by learning some intricate exercise or by spending years or thousands of trainer-dollars to unravel the mysteries of some dark, mystical phenomena (such as "collection" or "throughness"), but rather by making a few small and simple corrections that can make "all the difference" in not months, weeks or years - but minutes. What follows then, are a handful of subtle changes you can make to improve your riding in short order. I'm a big believer in the concept that a "one percent improvement" each day means a one hundred percent improvement in just three months and ten days - so take heed, little changes add up to big improvements. 1) When riding, we can (or should) only work on one thing at a time. (Not per ride, but at any given moment.) Example: You want to teach your horse to move diagonally to the right, but instead of moving his shoulders away from your left rein, he turns to the left. Here's incorrect: You quit asking for "diagonal" and take a moment to steer the horse back onto your "original path." You're thinking "We'll start over." The horse is thinking "Right, left, straight, move here, move there, make up your mind." You're confusing the devil out of your horse. Now, correct: If your horse mistakenly turns to the left, keep your pressure, and concentrate on causing those feet to move diagonally against your new path. Do not stop and reposition the horse. Know from the outset that you'll end up meandering all about the pen.

2) Stop riding dead-headed and start noticing things. Study the mechanics of your horse: "When I do this, I get that" or "This is always followed by that." Save these random scraps of knowledge, compile them, chew them over, and begin consciously collecting training snippets you can put into place not just today, but tomorrow or the next day. Dissect things: If you notice that your mare moves her hip (sideways, a "turn on the forehand") better to the right, than the left, then look down and ask yourself what's different between the two sides? If I made the bad side look like the good side before asking for the movement, would I have better luck? In this case, if you see that she naturally carries her shoulder more to the left (and therefore her hip more to the right), experiment to see if this natural stance is what's making the difference. Can you improve the "off side" with lessons learned from the "good side"? Try by first asking the shoulders to move slightly to the right (to reflect the body positioning on the "good side"), then ask for the hips to move to the left. You can cut out the stutter step you've added later when the horse understands your cue, but in the meantime, you've gotten your point across by using your brain.

Tip: Thinking as described is the real difference between a professional horse trainer and the casual rider. Too many riders think "My horse is a jerk and won't pick up the correct lead." A pro diagnoses the problem: "This horse won't pick up his left lead because he won't move his hips to the left. I'll gain that control through exercises a, b and c." Learn to break things down and to see the true "limiting factor" and you'll start fixing these issues yourself.

3) Begin collecting a list in your brain of "what's more important" for any horse handling situation. How many times have you set out to teach one thing - only to have something else fall apart? Should you ignore the new problem or fall back in your training and deal with it right away? That's where experience comes in and why I'm suggesting that you build this "Compendium of What's More Important."

An example: You begin working on hip control - but the horse keeps moving slower and slower. Any energy you had is quickly disappearing. Maybe the horse just plain stops. Is it more important to keep with the task at hand ("That hip's gotta move no matter what") or to deal with the speed issue? (An aside: Horses naturally slow down every time we pick up the reins. Teaching them to move through this pressure is absolutely necessary.) In the situation described, your priority should be speed control. Forget the hips momentarily. Get the horse moving out immediately and obligingly - then return to the hips. Because, simply put, you need movement to train. If you're working on hip control today, but at any time feel the horse "not moving out," then back off on your rein pressure and/or "goose" with your legs as necessary to get that horse moving fluidly. Take this a step further: If today we learn that movement is our priority when training those hips, remember this tomorrow when you're working on the shoulders.

4) Release your pressure on the thought, not the action. Trust me here, when you read this, you'll think, "Yeah, makes sense, okay." But sometime in the future, you'll be riding and this simple suggestion will hit you like a ton of bricks: "Holy guacamole, THAT'S what he was talking about. Genius!" As simple as it sounds, it's really one of the greatest concepts I've come across in horse training, (thanks to Josh Lyons), it's just that

important. Following faithfully this one easy rule will so simplify, galvanize and improve your training that you'll want to put a statue of me up in your room. In a nutshell, it's this: Don't hold the rein pressure till the horse actually plants his leg here or there or moves his body like this or that. Instead, release when you think the horse understands your request and is ABOUT to comply. Think of it this way: If you bat a ball at a window - when do you know it's going to break the glass? Do you wait till the glass actually hits the floor before you run? Or as the ball first touches the window? Or when you see that "If it keeps going in that direction it's going to break the window"? From now on, release the reins when you think the ball's sure to break the window.

There are several reasons for prescribing this: One, releasing sooner tells the horse more clearly what it is that caused the release. Less interim time means fewer things for the horse to consider: "Did I get a release because I dropped my head, because that guy scratched his nose or because that fly landed on my ear?" Two, releasing when the horse "is thinking correctly" is an easier thought process for us humans than releasing after we've gone through a checklist: "A) Flicka stepped correctly. Check. B) Flicka softened her neck. Check. C) I have Flicka's attention. Check. D) Flicka's attitude is good..." Blah, blah, blah... Three, releasing on the thought keeps us from "picking apart" the horse's actions. I asked the foot to step there. The horse understood and did just that. But maybe the head is slightly out of alignment and I continued to hold the reins - and, in so doing, I've just muddied the waters and confused the horse. Releasing on the thought MAKES YOU keep things simple. (Try it - it makes training a whole lot more fun.)

5) Take notice of the speed control you have through your transitions. The control you have as your horse moves from a trot up and into his lope or as your horse goes from walking ahead to backing up is a telltale sign. It's a major indicator of just how much compliance and understanding you have not just at that particular moment - but it telegraphs just what's going to happen when something spooks it on the trail or when you ask for a movement in the show pen. In other words, resistance under restrained circumstances grows exponentially worse when emotions run high. The very next time you ride, test your horse. Does it lift up into the lope like butter - or does it throw its shoulder and rush things? Can you be trotting forward and get a backup with virtually no stop in between - or do you have to finagle, threaten and negotiate? For safety's sake, if for no other reason, you need to address this: If your horse takes 10 feet to stop at a trot, he'll take 40 at a lope. If the cliff comes up in 39, you're toast. Reading the signs today can save your bacon tomorrow.

Work on this. Get out there and build total control through your transitions. Take the "stop" out of your back ups. Practice for twenty minutes walking or trotting forward, then backing, working furtively to remove any trace of a "stop." For twenty minutes you're either walking forward or backward. Keep things calm and business-like. Practice moving from a walk into a trot (and later from a trot to a lope and any other combination you can think of). Ask for speed and don't allow your horse to break into the trot until his head and neck are soft, (read: He ain't pullin' on the reins). Give the horse a slight release any time he softens through the reins, a total release if you get into the trot with a soft head and neck. If he wants to pull through your rein pressure, ask him to move his hips left or right. They're not crazy about moving their big ol' butts, so it's a great disincentive. Practice till your horse weighs nothing as he speeds up or down or changes direction. He doesn't lunge ahead, he doesn't pull on you, his attitude is patient.

6) Today your horse might believe that you expect him to move in one of three, four or five speeds: "Walk, trot, lope, run like hell." But this isn't true. In fact, he has an infinite amount of speeds that we might request - and he needs to learn this. A trot shouldn't always mean "4 mph." It might mean 4, 14 or 6.345 if I so desire. This is a big deal. Building in unlimited speeds does more than simply give you "more gears from which to choose." It also brings about far more willingness (and hence control) from your horse. To borrow a line from "Cool Hand Luke," it goes a long way to "getting their mind right." In the same way that controlling the colt's direction in the round pen builds respect, building excellent speed control into the older horse seems to have a parallel and positive effect on the horse's brain. They go from "going through the paces," to really being in tune with their rider.

While there are as many speed control exercises as there are trainers, you can create your infinite gear box like this: Pick up a trot and egg your horse into the fastest trot he'll trot before breaking into a lope. If he breaks into the lope, (and he will because it's actually easier for him), just bring him back to that fast trot with pressure to the reins. Travel for forty or so feet, then sit down, push your feet and weight down onto the horse's back and through the stirrups... and think "slow." Always begin your requests by changing your body or seat position (so it becomes your cue), then follow up if need be by adding necessary pressure to the reins or squeezing/kicking with your legs. Now you want to see the slowest the horse will trot before falling into a walk. (Remember, you need to "make mistakes" here in order to see what the boundaries are so expect them and accept them.) When you establish that your horse's slowest speed is "x" and the fastest is "y," work to broaden the boundaries. Do what it takes to cause your horse to travel at "x-1" or "y+1." While you're doing that, you'll additionally find yourself with ever greater control of all the speeds in between.

Rider Checklists

Here are 3 "Rider Checklists." Together, they'll keep you safer - and accelerate your training to boot.

When we don't have an objective means of approaching our training, when we simply "ride," reacting emotionally to what's happening, we're asking for a wreck - or at the very least, a bad day. The horse gets confused and we get frustrated or lose our temper. Not an environment conducive to a proper education, would you say?

Each of the following lists will cover small things you can simply check off in your brain. Basically, has something happened or not? If the answer is "not," I'll tell you what to do. Your answers to those questions will, flowchart-like, tell you how to act in the moment or how best to form your day's game plan.

The lists were created to "be done in order."

Checklist 1: How To Keep From Totally Losing It

Before you ever get on your horse, back when you're approaching the barn, ask yourself one easy question: "Am I training today or am I joyriding?" If you answer "training," skip to Checklist Two. If you answered "Uh,

I'd like a day off from training, please. I got a horse to have FUN, Mr. Wet Blanket Trainer Man" - that's great, too. It's great as long as you can honestly say that not once in the last few days or months have you turned to a friend and said something akin to "Flicka nearly bucked my teeth out back there" or "This (expletive deleted) horse keeps trying to eat grass. What's the number for the tiger sanctuary?" If there are known issues, then it doesn't matter where you ride (trail or arena), the fact is, you need to be training as opposed to joyriding.

At clinic after clinic, here in the states or in Europe, I get a version of the same question: "I'm out on the trail. On a cliff. With a ten thousand foot drop to my right and cactus on the left. My horse hates plastic bags - but one blows by and he freaks. What do I do?" To which I answer something akin to "Say your prayers." See, training is not a widget that you carry in your back pocket and pull out like a parachute when the plane goes down. It's about practice and preparation. Ignoring warning signs and riding into potential disaster is like eating a cake every night and suddenly freaking when the scale reads "300."

If riding your horse has become an aggravation or something that - even at times - frightens you, then you gotta answer "training" until riding is fun again. Following this simple thought process will have a bigger impact than if I told you to specifically do a, b, or c - because there are trillions of horse/rider combinations and situations that might be described. So, with a nod to the ol' John Lyons axiom "Ride Where You Can, Not Where You Can't," we'll consciously pick a reasonably safe place to do our training and get at it. Example One: Is your horse "jiggy"? Then you need to capture his attention by improving his performance. How do you do that? By being a proactive rider. Keep giving the horse something to do. Make him spin enough plates and he'll hand you control. Example Two: Does your horse keep munching grass? Then develop a zero-tolerance policy toward any resistance on the part of your horse. Be on the lookout for resistance in the form of a stiff neck or a horse that won't move forward when asked. Don't wait till his head's on the ground. Test constantly and the instant you feel reticence, correct the situation. If you feel an ounce of stiffness in the neck, apply pressure and get the horse moving till he relaxes, then you relax. Teach the horse that the way to get you out of his mouth is to stay soft and obliging. The answer is the same if he drops to a speed you didn't ask for. Be ready with a good kick and swift reward. If you just thought to yourself: "That's what I do and it doesn't work" then what's happening is that you're keeping pressure on the horse's mouth all the time (example one) or kicking all the time (example two). The horse has learned "I get punished no matter what I do so I might as well do what I wanna do." Learn to be more aware of when you're applying pressure. It doesn't matter what you think you're doing, your horse's actions tell a different story.

Checklist 2: The Best Advice I Will Ever Give You

Emotion is a wonderful thing when the sensation you're experiencing is "elation" - but it's a total bummer when you're feeling "anger" or "frustration." In that respect riding can be truly feast or famine. I'll explain: As rider/trainers, we've got great days and we've got "blech" days. A blech day happens when we allow our emotions to creep into our training. The horse doesn't get it or just doesn't give a darn and we get angry. That's bad mojo there - because what happens is that anger causes us to let go of the reins not when the horse simply gives to pressure - but after we've "really made our point." Or to give them an extra kick after they've sped up to "really teach them not to slow down." Things go from bad to worse and we walk back to the barn dejected. We spend the rest of the day depressed or wondering what we're doing with a horse in the first place.

But you can have a great day every day! A great day is any day that we make an improvement, however small, and keep our negative emotions in check. Doing so will keep you and your horse on the same page and build a positive relationship. Get busy with your training and react objectively to any roadblock your horse (or nature) might erect and you'll find yourself enjoying the heck out of riding that day.

So Checklist Two only has one question on it: Are you keeping things objective - or letting negative emotion creep into your reactions? Notice the word "reactions" in that last sentence. Becoming emotional puts you in a position of reacting rather than being proactive. That's a downhill slide. The horse misunderstands something and you react by jerking the reins. The horse reacts to that by bracing and stiffening up. Break this cycle: Every so often as you ride, take stock of the situation. Are you staying calm and methodical? Are you trying your level-best to break things down into their simplest form? Or are you beginning to blame the horse? Blaming the horse is a pretty good sign we're not being rational. Get off and walk around, cool out. Ask yourself if you couldn't break down your lesson even more. Then give it another shot.

The single best advice I can ever give you in the world of horse training comes into play right here: No matter what your horse (or the day) throws at you, learn to find joy in it. Short of getting kicked in the head, you've got to react to your horse's reaction by smiling and telling yourself two things. One, your horse has given you a gift; he's told you exactly what you need to work on. No more wondering "What do I do today"? He's told you. Two, well, there is no "two." Go back and re-read number one. It all boils down to this: Approaching your riding with "We're going to do what I want to do" is asking for trouble. Riding with the attitude of "Horse, what would you like to work on?" will keep you forever in a positive frame of mind. You will enjoy your horse's company; he will enjoy yours.

Checklist 3:
When Can I Get Medieval On Ol' Dobber?

Whether you're leading, feeding, roundpenning, riding or just hanging out at the barn, there should always be "two versions of you" out there with the horse. One of you is Dr. Jekyll the other, Mr. Hyde. Dr. Jekyll is the nice guy, the one who everybody loves, the life of the party. He's patient, easy-going, fun and kind. Still, nobody messes with him. Why? Because of his close relationship with Mr. Hyde. Mess with Jekyll and Hyde comes out of nowhere, delivering his punishment, vanishing quickly.

But when is punishment called for? Smacking your horse randomly isn't going to win you hearts and minds - and, conversely, letting poor behavior slide is a non-starter.

The answer comes from asking yourself this: "Is my horse trying?"

If your horse is getting things wrong - but is trying - then no punishment is called for. Not ever. You can't punish him even if what he's doing is wrong, wrong, wrong, again and again and again. ("Punishment" is any sort of punitive action, from adding pronounced pressure to the reins to spurring, from screaming obscenities to using a crop.) If he's trying, you keep asking until he finally stumbles upon the answer or you find another way to ask. Patience is the rule here. Your horse is teaching you to be a better trainer (because you'll find yourself motivated to search for more effective communication). Fortunately, he can only go 6 directions (up, down, left, right, etc.) so we know he'll get the answer sooner or later if we stay consistent. Keep Dr. J locked up.

If, by contrast, you believe that your horse simply isn't trying, try "making the wrong thing uncomfortable" as Clinton Anderson likes to say. Stave off the use of crop or spur by instead making the horse work harder: Try speeding him up. Try asking for a different movement entirely, one that calls for a larger expenditure of energy such as moving his hips if he's not willing to move his shoulders. Don't get into an argument, use that big ol' brain of yours.

Finally, if your horse isn't trying, if he's just locked you out and you've tried extra motivation as outlined with few to zero results, then consciously change your persona until your horse decides to begin working with you: Become Mr. Hyde. If before, you were patient and forgiving, now you are militant, uncompromising and exacting. You don't nag; you use decisive, telling, pressure on the reins when you pick them up and do everything a tad more quickly. Be strict. Be stern. Offer little-to-no benefit of the doubt. Ask for a maneuver once nicely and if you get nothing, ramp up your pressure quickly to jolt him awake and say "quit messing around." Use your spur or bat if need be (and do so in a business-like fashion). Convince the horse that he's picked up a new rider, one that expects results. The very instant you feel the horse's demeanor turn back in your favor, return to your old, tolerant, forgiving (Dr. Jeckyll) self.

The First Thing I Do

Here's the first thing you should do with your horse today - and with any horse that's "new to you."

What's the first thing I do when I meet a new horse? The same thing you should do with your horse today and everyday: Give them a "resistance test." If you have the typical horse - whether you'd call him a problem child or a good horse with just "occasional challenges" - this is for you.

If you get one thing from reading this material, it should be this: Any resistance from your horse while he's hanging out, just standing next to you munching grass, will be many times worse when things get hairy. If it takes one pound of pressure today to get him leading (away from that grass), it'll take one hundred when he gets spooked on the trail.

You have to ferret out those "one pound moments" and eradicate them like weeds. They're seeds that can grow into major disasters very quickly on the trail. If your horse "only freaks out once or twice a year but is otherwise great" - then you're fooling yourself. You're overlooking slip ups from your horse, perhaps on a daily basis, that will sooner or later get you hurt. Remember, accidents are by their very nature "things we don't expect."

If your horse went ballistic out on the trail last week... it didn't "just happen out of the blue." He's been telling you for weeks or months that he was going to lose it when enough pressure was applied and he said this every time he resisted however slightly the pull from your lead rope or reins.

If he walks ahead of you while you lead him, he's telling you that sooner or later he'll blow past you as you go through a gate or knock you on your kiester with his shoulder when something scares him bad enough.

If the muscles in his neck bulge toward you instead of relaxing when you put the bit in his mouth, he's telling you that he'll do mach sixty when he gets spooked on the trail.

Deal with these situations by doing two things: First establish a zero-tolerance policy; nip bad behavior in the bud the instant it happens. Example: If your horse inches past you as you lead, do an about-face and back that horse up. Keep him moving till he quits pushing back. (If he freezes pull on his head to pull his butt away from you. Getting those feet "unstuck" will allow you to keep backing till he lightens up.) Be adamant.

Second, get proactive. The first thing I do with any horse - and what I do each and everyday with all five of my own horses - is to see exactly where they stand when it comes to "resistance." Luckily the test and remedy are fun.

And having fun with this is a key point. Realize that every horse has resistance tucked away somewhere. Like an Easter egg, your job is to discover it. Instead of chocolate, your reward is a safer, more pleasant ride. The calmest, coolest, bestest trained horse you have ever seen has a little pocket of resistance hidden somewhere. Ever see that great comedy "The Ref"? Dennis Leary needs a cigarette bad. When he's told that actress Judy Davis has given up smoking, he smiles and asks her where her secret stash is. Being a smoker, he knows she's got one or two hidden somewhere in the house for high-stress moments.

In a like way, your horse may be a real pleasure 99% of the time, but somewhere inside him he's got resistance tucked away for "high-stress moments."

So let's get started squashing rebellion. Approach your horse from his left (bridled, haltered, bare naked, it matters not) and place your left hand across the bridge of his nose, about six inches below his eyes. Look at the horse's neck and pick out the area where the muscle is bulging and not relaxed. Place your right index finger on that spot and pull a little (toward yourself) on the nose with your left hand. Your left hand should pull with a pressure roughly equivalent to the weight of three TV remote controls, (might as well use a standard we're all familiar with). It's important that your horse doesn't feel trapped; you're not wrestling. He should be able to pull away from your grasp.

He'll most likely pull away and when he does simply put him back into position by pulling again on the nose. (Your index finger should have stayed in place; don't allow it to fall away when your horse moves off.) Keep putting the horse back into position till he just kinda "stays put."

The instant you feel the muscle (via your index finger) relax in the slightest let the horse go completely and pet heavily. Repeat this simple piece of business until his neck looks and feels completely relaxed.

One of the things this accomplishes is lateral flexion. Lateral flexion is a fancy way of saying your horse bends from left to right (as opposed to vertical flexion, which is "up and down"). Here's the other major point you should take from reading this; underline the following in your brain: Your horse won't get "soft" vertically (drop his head, collect up, etc.) if he is isn't soft laterally. (And when I use the word "soft" I mean "relaxed.")

Perhaps you've read this many times before, but it bears repeating: It's not the movements you ask your horse to do (back up, move a shoulder, etc.) that are hard. What makes it hard is the resistance. Your horse can no more perform a smooth sidepass when the two of you are fighting than Frankenstein (with his stiff movements) can win "Dancing with the Stars."

Where does the resistance come from? Lots of places. Could be years of having his mouth yanked on (go put a spoon in your mouth and let somebody yank on it) or maybe, in the case of a young, green horse, he just resists 'cause nature has programmed him to. Try this: Walk up to somebody with your palm facing them and suggest (with your body language) that they place their palm against yours. Now push. They'll (99 out of 100 times) push back. Ask them why they did so and they'll have no idea. Your horse is the same way.

If by some strange quirk your horse's neck is completely soft and Gumby-like from the beginning, skip to the next step, which is: Apply pressure to the horse's "forehead," asking it to drop, in effect moving closer to his body. (His forehead will become more perpendicular to the ground.) When you get that, ask for the head to bend toward you again. This time place your entire right arm over the horse's neck. (His neck will be "in" your armpit.) Be careful not to place your head/mouth directly over the horse in such a way that if he came up quickly he'd bash you in the mouth. That's a good way to lose teeth. Keep your teeth. Don't get over the horse even for an instant.

Initially your horse will resist by pushing his head up in the air or by trying to pull away. Keep putting him back in position. Release any and all pressure any time you feel the horse relax, however slight. (Usually they'll just sort of "drop" below you.) Your "goal position" should be to get the horse to stand, completely relaxed, with his head and neck wrapped around your chest with your arms virtually draped over the horse. At this point your demeanor should be relaxed, business-like, non-threatening and with an attitude that suggests "I've got all day."

You're on an Easter egg hunt, looking for pockets of hidden resistance. You know they're there - find them by progressively moving faster or by bending your horse into more "creative" positions. It takes time, but as your horse begins to relax for longer moments, hang on a bit longer. Push the envelope, so to speak.

As your horse becomes more accustomed to you hanging on him, (perhaps in moments, perhaps weeks) your attitude should begin alternating between business-like (as we've practiced so far) and that of the older sister giving the younger brother a noogie. Playful, a little rough, but not disrespectful or mean spirited.

Keep the sister-annoying-the-younger-brother theme in mind; get creative and have fun. If others in your barn don't think you've gone a tad loopy, you're not having enough fun. Jump around, hang around your horse's neck, push him around with your rear end. Spin around and sing a show tune. Use common sense here. After all, the younger sister's gonna get tossed out of the back of the car if she gets too annoying.

Caution: Only pet your horse when it's emotions go down, never when they're going up. If he gets excited and his head flares up, put your arm around his nose and apply pressure till he relaxes however slightly. Then pet. (And you may want to ratchet down your own energy level a bit.) Petting your horse "to calm him" is like saying "There, there, it's good to be scared." He doesn't have to be dead calm to get the pet, just "calmer."

Do you realize what you're doing with this exercise? You're changing your horse's first impulse (when pressured) from resistance to softness. Think about it: Hanging on his neck with your hand is no different than pulling on his mouth with a bit. It's just a bit safer, pun intended. Practice and build on this until you can jump around, move fast and "be a bit jarring" and you'll be strengthening your horse's "emotion muscle" in a controlled situation. Remember, if you want your horse to withstand 100 pounds of pressure out on the trail (when a car backfires or the other horses take off), you have to start by making him strong enough to withstand just one pound.

For those of you with scared rabbit horses, you can really build on this. As time goes by, you can create 20, 50 and 80 pound moments by finding progressively more scary places to do your work. Today, do what I described (above) in your pasture. When your horse gives like a soggy noodle, go find an "outside influence" like the local park where your horse will be a bit more amped - and practice the same there. If you begin today in your own arena (1 pound), maybe next week or month you'll be next to the freeway (40 pounds) and a month after that you'll be walking/riding past the barking dog (80). In the example I just gave, all the steps between the freeway and the barking dog represents new numbers and places to work. The numbers, of course, are guesstimates and highly relative, but you get the idea.

When You Get On, Do This First

Here's one small thing you can do to keep your horse's attitude in check - and prevent mount-up problems from taking root.

Each time you get on your horse, get in the habit of just sitting there relaxing for half a minute or so. Drape the reins loosely around your horse's neck, one of your hands holding the reins there against his mane/withers. Slouch down and take a moment to enjoy the view. Breathe deep and listen to the birds, check out the coming sunset or plan out your next home improvement. When thirty seconds tick by, pick up the reins and ask your horse to walk off. This is especially important if you're running late or in a bad mood.

Why the pause? Because forcing yourself to "cool it" for a bit will force you into neutral and away from the "go go go" you might be feeling after rushing to the barn and tacking up. Rather than barging into things (and perhaps taking "things" out on your horse), establish a rhythm and pace for your ride that's calm, rational and thought-out. You're not simply "trying to get this over with."

And, do this because you don't want your horse in the habit of moving off on his own. After all, what's the point of going out and working on brakes or speed control - when your horse began the session by ignoring this very thing?

If your horse is already in the habit of walking off as you mount up, then he's either scared (most likely of your hands and how you use your reins) - or he's disrespecting you (or both). Allowing your horse to call the shots in such a way eats away at any respect you might have gained previously and often goes from bad to worse.

The first time he tries this, you can simply back him up a few paces and give him another shot at standing still. If he doesn't learn to stand "right quick," then allow him to walk off - and work him intensely (serpentines, diagonals, speed control - anything) for twenty full minutes before giving him the option to stand again. Make him see that standing is a better option. Also, get better with your hands. You may very well be applying pressure to his mouth (too much or at the wrong times) without realizing it. Watch yourself (or have a friend/trainer watch you). Study your pick up and release of the reins and see if you can't back off on all that pressure.

Nutshell: Get on your horse and sit there for thirty seconds because it sets your overall pace and because it objectively proves that the horse is waiting for your command not "taking over." If he moves off, work intensely for twenty minutes and give him another chance to stand. Also, make an effort to get lighter with your hands, releasing sooner.

Is My Horse Hard to Train... Because of His Feet?

If your horse stumbles, cranes his head to the ground, takes halting steps, doesn't want to "move out," or has grown irritable, it might be that his feet are hurting him. Here's how to tell.

Does your horse stumble or trip a lot? Or pitch his head forward and down, almost to the ground in a sort of spoiled teenager fashion as he trots along? Does he take small, dicey steps in his jog and feel like he's reluctant to "move out"? Is the horse that used to be willing and fun now irritable? Are these things getting worse almost daily?

Your horse might very well be doing these things because his feet hurt. And if it's because his feet hurt, then see this as a sign that you need to get your farrier out more often. It might be that his every step causes pain because he's either due for a trim -- or the spacing between his past trims has been too great -- and now the both of you are paying the piper. As easy as it is for us to dismiss this rather boring aspect of horse-having, don't you do it. It's not going away and it greatly effects your whole horse for obvious reasons.

It might be that your horse is off because he's gone too long between trims and developed a flaring out at the bottom of his hoof that causes him pain with each step. (Sort of like when you pull a finger nail back unnaturally. More on this in a moment.) Flares are common and easily remedied with more frequent, quality hoof care. It might also be, however, that your horse has developed toes that are too long and heels that are too sensitive. His heels hurt and he's begun protecting them by landing "toe first." You need to know that, left unchecked, "toe first landings" will eventually put your horse out of commission entirely. The good news is that this is also remedied by more frequent trims -- but it's going to take more time to fix this -- and the farrier may very well prescribe that your horse wear protective boots in order to give the "hoof capsules" a chance to heal themselves.

First, flare: Horses have evolved in such a way that their hooves are designed to grow down and be continually worn off by active movement from the horse as he travels mile after mile in the wild eating and running and doing what horses do. No need for farriers as long as they travel many miles each day. In complete contrast, however, when we keep a horse in a stall and neglect regular trimming, his body knows that hoof horn isn't being worn off -- and it begins constructing thinner walls. It creates thin walls because weaker walls are more easily broken off. Further, these neglected hooves don't keep "growing down" or truly forgotten horses would be walking six inches off the ground. What they do is to flare out like a bell -- and then eventually break off. (In more extreme cases, this natural defense can't keep up and the hoof will continue to grow till the horse can't even stand up.) When your farrier keeps your horse's feet trimmed with regularity, he's "fooling" the feet into thinking the hoof is being worn off in a natural fashion so the hooves remain thick and strong.

It's a pretty amazing system -- but it can be painful when the horse takes a step and that flared-out section hangs first on a rock before the rest of the hoof lands on the ground. That rock, coupled with the horse's weight and movement, will cause the hoof "horn" to be pulled away from the hoof. The horse feels pain -- and might very well end up with a crack or chip that only grows worse. Consider how many times this very thing is going to happen on an average training session. How many times would you bite into a sandwich with a bad tooth before you started acting in the same halting fashion as your horse?

Even the layperson can see "flare" for himself: Look at the top of your horse's "hoof capsule" there at the coronet/hair band. Reach down and wrap your thumb and forefinger around the hoof, one inch down from the coronet band/hair line in such a way that your blocking the rest of the hoof and looking at just this upper section. Now, pull your hand away. Does the hoof (at any point, all the way around) continue down to the ground at the angle you'd expect based on the first inch -- or does it buckle away? Any flare you might see is evidence that the hoof has been allowed to grow too long. There's your proof to yourself that you need to see your farrier more often. Depending on the severity, you might be looking at months -- or give or take a year -- for this to grow out and "reattach" so you can see that putting off that trim has lasting ramifications.

Your horse might have bigger issues than simply a bit of flare. When a horse's hoof wall grows too long, it lifts the bottom of the foot off the ground and prevents other parts of the foot from helping to absorb impact, structures like the frog, bars and sole. This, of course, stresses out the very structure of the hoof because one "part" isn't supposed to do all the work. Hold your right sleeve with your left hand and pull the sleeve toward your elbow. This is what happens to the horse's feet as the horse "falls through" to the ground because the walls are too long and the other structures are not able to share the load.

For the frog's part, when the walls grow too long and lift it off the ground, the frog tends to shrivel up. The horse needs a good healthy frog because it offers protection from the outside world -- but also because it (and the structure above it) helps absorb the impact as the foot strikes the ground. Your horse will land heel first (at gaits faster than a walk) when his feet are in good shape; he'll land toe first when his heels hurt in an effort to avoid pressuring the back half of his foot which is causing him pain. When he starts doing this, things go from bad to worse. A vicious cycle develops. With each step he takes, favoring his toe over his heel, the internal structures fall apart -- literally. What happens is a long, flowchart-like sequence of events that all add up to a lame horse.

(Note that the frog can also cause the horse pain all by itself when it takes on an infection such as "thrush," so be ever-vigilant for evidence of nasty bacteria or fungus in this area in particular. If the frog becomes infected you might try using a 60cc catheter-tip syringe to squirt in a 50-50 mix of common athlete's foot cream and "triple antibiotic" ointment into the cleft. Do it daily to eradicate the issue. You can pick up both products over the counter at any pharmacy; get the syringe from your vet.)

If you take nothing from this material but one thing, learn that allowing your horse's feet to go unmaintained will do damage that takes a great deal of time to remedy. Any money you save by skipping trims will never be worth the "down time" the both of you will face to fix all this in the coming future. Find a way to get his feet done, even if it means learning how to do it yourself.

If you take two things, know this: Even the horse that's "out to pasture" needs to have his feet done in a timely fashion. Don't think "He's not doing anything but lounging; we can skip a trim or two." (I fell for that lame logic and it's why I'm writing this now, hoping to save you the same pain.) Pasture horses (brood mares, retirees, youngsters, etc.) need to have their feet looked after just as a working horse does. Otherwise, if you let things go and later bring them in to begin working with them, you may very well find that you're gonna have to wait about a year until they're one hundred percent again.

The bottom line is that, as equestrians, we need to be aware of how our horse's movements (and attitude) can directly reflect what's happening "under the hood." Before blaming our horse for having a bad attitude or simply being a brat, we need to consider whether he's got a legitimate gripe. Make an effort to schedule some time soon with your farrier to discuss any issues your horse might have developed in the ring. Are your horse's movements being compromised for any reason he can see? A horse might be "off" for a myriad of factors that a farrier is best suited to spot, (some worse than what I'll describe here) so the consultation will surely be worth your time. Do it sooner rather than later because the more you allow things to deteriorate, the longer it'll take to fix -- and the more expensive it'll be.

Section III: Overt Vices

Here's how to fix some of the most common problems you might face with your horse: Easy, objective, step-by-step

Horses That Bite

Biting is the worst vice your horse can have. It's more dangerous than bucking, than rearing, than kicking -- more dangerous than anything else you can name. Here's what to do.

A horse can nip off a finger, an ear or objects I'd rather not mention in an instant. He can do so without warning and lightning fast. Greased lightning fast. He's a prey animal with the reflexes of a prey animal.

Prevention is your first line of defense when it comes to biting. Know that your horse would never, ever bite its own mother and see this as an issue of a horse that does not respect its human. Turn that dynamic around by setting up a zero-tolerance policy to disrespect shown by your horse. Watch for moments when you are being treated with disregard and deal with infractions immediately. When you walk from A to B and your horse blocks your path, he gets out of your way, not the other way around. When you feed, you don't walk off if your horse rushes up rudely, bullying with his shoulders. Instead, you set him back -- literally and figuratively. When he pins his ears as you buckle the halter, put him to work at once and do so intensely. Do any ground work exercise you know, for ten or so minutes; show him that tranquility can only be had when deference is shown. A good thing to do in any case is to simply back your horse. Back him up for a football field or two and remind him that you pay the bills.

If he's begun biting, or he's "mouthy" and you fear it might morph into something more aggressive, then do each of the following to protect yourself:

1) Until and unless your horse becomes a model citizen, allow him no time to stand around looking for problems to cause. When he's with you, find him a job and keep him busy. Practice any ground maneuvers you'd like to make better. Ask him to move his shoulders, to back, to disengage his hind end... anything, just keep him busy.

2) This goes without saying, but a reminder couldn't hurt: Keep your horse's teeth consciously positioned away from you when he's in your presence. The easiest and most objective way to do this is to insist that he stay a few feet away from you at all times. Have your safe zone and insist that he maintain his distance.

3) Any time the horse gets mouthy, in fact, anytime you even think he's thinking about it, recall the cartoon character Peppy LePew. Specifically recall the classic episode when Peppy (a skunk) fell in love with the black cat. She couldn't stand him. He'd hug her tightly, oblivious to her wriggling frantically to get away. He was in love; she thought he stunk. Literally.

To fix your biting horse, you'll be Peppy LePew and your horse the cat. Start looking for excuses to hug and love on him like Peppy did that cat. The next time he signals his displeasure at anything, even for an instant, drop what you're doing, take his nose between your hands and pet and pet and pet. Pet him until he takes his head away -- and then grab it back and do it some more.

Push your horse a little. Dare him to show aggravation -- and the moment he does, give him all the attention he seems to be looking for and more; pet him feverishly and until he screams "enough!" and tries to pull away. Have fun with it and look for opportunities to do it. Doing so makes you "active." No longer are you waiting for an attack. Now you're in the driver's seat -- now you get respect.

Tip: This same "fix" works with horses that act like jerks when cinched up. The next time you pull the cinch tight and the horse responds by throwing his head up, dancing around or gnashing his teeth, try taking his muzzle in your hands and rubbing it incessantly. (If your horse reacts negatively to the sight of your saddle, first make sure that it fits correctly and not causing him pain. Don't expect him to "get over" a painful fit.)

The beauty of this method is this: First, acting like the teasing older sister or brother, antagonizing your horse, is just plain fun. Second, you'll see that the horse you once feared anytime it nosed around, now minds his own business, hoping you don't notice him and start getting all weird again.

Cinchy Horses

Here's an easy fix for horses that get cinchy or irritated when you tack up.

Have you ever seen a film that took place in a prison in which the prisoners didn't have some sort of secret world? Every prison film details the "secret life" the population carries on, the guards (seemingly) oblivious. They've got a whole "underground railroad" thing happening - with goods and services flowing back and forth, even their own currency. (Isn't it always cigarettes?) The underlying current making this all possible, of course, is their secret pipeline of communication, secret signals, informants and couriers, their own unique language. One tap of a tin can means the guard is coming, that sort of thing. The warden locks up for the night, hands the keys to his next-in-charge and goes home to the wife and kids. Meanwhile, prisoners 001 and 3924 are hatching some evil scheme to heist egg noodles from the kitchen.

Well, if your horse is stabled with one or more equine friend, he's doing the same. (Keeping him in "solitary" has it's own issues. "Cribbing" and "weaving" come to mind.) The very moment your car pulls out of the drive they get down to concocting their mischief. Maybe it's a feed room break in, maybe they're gonna kick a door in, maybe somebody's getting roughed up. One thing is absolutely certain, the older, more experienced horses are spending their evening counseling the others on ways to drive us nuts. "Move right before they put their foot in the stirrup." (Big horse laughs here) "That's a good one." I've got seven horses of my own and I know without a doubt that they get together and pass along what works, what doesn't, and how to make me crazy.

It certainly doesn't take them long to learn that a saddle on their backs means they're getting put to work pretty quick - so it's no wonder that so many bad habits develop along this point. They weren't born yesterday: You approaching with a smile on your face, a saddle in one hand and "Riding for Newbies" in the other can only mean one thing: Work. It's no wonder they begin channeling the advice they've heard from their buddies: "Dance around," "Act like you're gonna bite," "Don't let him put the bit in your mouth. You get a bit in your mouth and you're done for." And, they're always trying something new, aren't they? I'd finally worked one of my mares through - what I thought was every bad habit at saddling time - only to have her lay down on me. (I cured this by being the ready the next time: The moment her legs began to buckle I screamed like a stuck pig and got her moving... anywhere. Trust me, she didn't go back and tell the others to try laying down.)

You can only deal with these crazy things they try in one way - and that's by keeping your sense of humor. They're going to keep coming like the tides - and the moment you lose your temper, they've got ya. Know why? Because your horse is dancing around, saying to himself "This is the part where he gets nuts everyday and smacks me." You lose your temper, smack the horse and prove him right. Every day. You do get the saddle on, the bit in his mouth - but each time it gets more difficult. Like the boy with his finger in the dike, new holes keep popping up.

Young horses, the ones being saddled for nearly the first time, pull garbage because they're young horses being saddled for the first time. Experienced horses are a pain at saddling time because they have owners who lose their tempers and make it a bigger deal than it is, owners who usually do nothing to dissuade the practice other than getting pissed. The ol "curse the darkness, rather than light a candle" school of training.

When we say "cinchy horse" what we're referring to is a horse that pins his ears, dances around or otherwise flips us the angry bird when we go to strap on the saddle. Every horse on the planet is going to try this at least once. Even the coolest horse is going to have a bad day and sooner or later react by grimacing at best, kicking or biting at worst, as the saddle tightens. It's natural and to be expected and not to be tolerated. You don't feel like going to work each and every day, do you? Does that give you license to kick your boss? Duh, no. As long as your horse has no girth sores or "hidden under the skin sore spots," he's gonna have to buck up, pardon the pun. Not dealing with this when they try it the first time leads to the same stunt being tried the next day. (And again, losing your temper and strapping them up anyway, without actually dissuading this bad habit, may also cause them to continue the behavior.)

Smacking the horse has actually worked for people. I'm not saying it doesn't or hasn't. The problem is, it doesn't work for me. I just don't have the timing it takes and only seem to make matters go from bad to worse. It's tough walking the fine line between punishment and abuse (in the horse's mind at least), you know?

Understand that your saddle (or cinch or bit or what-have-you) might actually be hurting your horse and that his sour attitude might simply be a reflection of pain he's feeling while being worked. And know this: Whatever's causing him pain may not be obvious to you. The bit you love could be pinching the corners of his mouth. Maybe he's developed sharp spots on his teeth or his "baby teeth" are clashing with the heavy bit. (Ask your vet.) The saddle that fits your seat might be too narrow on his shoulders, binding his movements. The best cinches out there can still chafe and leave nearly-hidden under-the-skin edemas. Adjusting your equipment and staying off your horse's back for a few days might be your remedy, so first rule out such physical - and understandable - causes.

Check anything and everything that comes into contact with your horse, sleuthing for something that might be rubbing your horse the wrong way... literally. Have the flies nibbled a hole on his underbelly, right where that cinch grabs? Do you see white hairs on his back? (They can represent a poor fit.) After riding, are the sweat spots on his back even - or spotty? (Uneven sweat spots equal an uneven fit.) Look for obvious open sores, rub your hands all over to feel for swellings or hot spots, use your fingers to feel for rough or pinching areas on your bit. (Note: Those rubberized, neoprene, cinches are easy for you to keep clean - but frequently cause sore spots on your horse's belly especially after long rides on hot days. Be alert to this. Check for any puffy spots under his skin where the cinch lies and remember they're hard to see, easier to feel). It should go without saying that if you find a sore spot, give your horse a short holiday, doctor any maladies, and switch out your gear - then vary the equipment used to see if you can't isolate the issue. Try a mohair cinch, a different saddle pad - or your neighbor's wider saddle. Rule out such physical - and understandable causes before you chalk up bad behavior to bad manners.

[Correct saddle and tack fit are hefty topics in their own right - well beyond the scope of this chapter. You should take any questions to a pro trainer, your vet, or local tack store. Go talk to someone "in the know."]

If I've ruled out pain as the underlying issue, I can reason that my horse is playing me - and so I need a way to motivate my horse to stand politely, a method that doesn't cause him to hate or fear me. Something simple, something foolproof, something that doesn't make me the bad guy.

Well, I actually have two somethings for you. First, if your horse wants to dance about as you tack up, then be ready the next time. Be ready to take the time it takes to fix this. You only think you're going to be riding the trail five minutes from now. The thousand pound animal you'd like to ride is telling you that he'd rather work on improving his ground manners. That's what you'll do: You'll begin seeing the dancing as "code" for "I'd like to improve my leading." Rather than actually tying your horse up, drape the lead line around the post and be ready. (I'm sure I don't have to tell you to make the correction as close to the time of the actual infraction as possible in order to make the connection in their brain.) The very moment you even think the horse is thinking of beginning his dance, take up the lead line and begin practicing your ground control. For the next ten minutes, ask the horse to back up or isolate his hips (move his head toward his hips causing the shoulder nearest you to stop while the hind end continues to move), side pass his shoulders... anything you can think of. Just keep the horse moving and improving. Give him a chance to stand politely and - when he blows it - put him back to work. Again and again until he realizes that it's easier to stand and be saddled than to "have a dance with you." (If he makes a move that you don't know how to read, that is you don't know if he actually dissed you, assume he did. That's the beauty of this versus smacking, it's thought-free and you can't lose.)

The fix for a horse that pins its ears is the same we'd use for a biter: We love our enemy because we know it kills 'em. Remember, were we to react by losing our temper, we're a) reacting as opposed to being proactive and b) telling the horse that he was right, we do start acting nuts every day at this time; he's right to be agitated when he sees a saddle. Instead, we need to begin looking forward to our horse "acting up" because it's an excuse to train. I promise that if you begin looking forward to your horse's shenanigans, as if they're Easter eggs and he's begging to practice his ground manners, you'll shortly find that your horse will just stand there, doing his level best to blend into the background.

What you'll do is simply this: Put your horse in a position that has - till now - caused him to pin an ear or otherwise grow agitated. Beg him, you want this. Be on the lookout and the moment you even think he's stiffened or given you the evil eye, take his muzzle between your two hands and rub it like Genie's lamp. You are the overbearing Aunt who comes to visit and hugs on you ad nauseum. (Hint on how to administer this fix: "Ad nauseum" is a Latin term for pushing something to the point of nausea.) She doesn't make you mad, you just tend to slink out of the room when you hear her pull up. The horse will pull his head away after a moment - you pull it back and repeat. See this as fun. Do this several times to make your point before releasing and going about your tack up. You'll need to repeat this process a few times and for perhaps a few days. Be on the lookout for the first time the horse begins to get agitated - but then suddenly thinks better of it. It's the funniest thing you're going to see for awhile.

No. The horse doesn't hold this against you. They do know the difference between affection and anger. And, to the contrary, establishing boundaries will improve your situation. (It's a whole "prey-animal-hierarchical thing." I'm sure you get the idea.)

And so that's all there is to it. We haven't made an issue out of anything. We didn't make matters worse. We didn't raise our blood pressure. Instead we dealt with the issue. We improved our training and the standing we have with our horse. And, we got to be little devils for a little while, which is always fun.

This simple method works by killing them with kindness. What's he gonna do? Go back and tell the other horses "I bit him 'cause he hugged on me?

Horses That Won't Go

Addressed here: Horses that stop moving and stubbornly refuse to take another step. Two things not addressed here (at least not in-depth or specifically): Horses that have gradually become "dead-sided" and crossing obstacles.

Warning 1): Putting pressure on a resistant horse's mouth, especially evenly with two reins, just might cause them to rear. Rearing is bad, real bad. It's one of the most dangerous things they can do - so don't ever foster that thought in your horse's head, not even for an instant. If you've got a horse that refuses to move forward, then you've got a potential rearing candidate. How and why? Because rearing is the ultimate case of "not moving forward." With this in mind, if you even sense that anything described here might cause your horse to get lighter in the front end, DON'T DO IT. Seek out how-to materials that explain how you can get better with your hands. Better: Attend a clinic. Best bet: Hire a pro. Hiring a professional horse trainer for several months is much cheaper than even a single trip to the emergency room.

Warning 2): Horses that lock up are sometimes signaling that the next step they take will be explosive. The methods described below pertain not so much to green horses with their nervous energy (or horses with a history of any dangerous habits, for that matter) as it does stubborn war horses who just seem to be playing you. You'll need to decide which horse you're riding, factor in common sense, and go forward accordingly. Again, hire a pro if there's a doubt.

"How do I get my horse to move when it freezes up?" I've heard this same question many times at clinics all over the US - and world, for that matter. (Odd but true: Every where I go to conduct a clinic, from the US, to Germany, even the Czech Republic... their citizens have the same horse-training issues as we do here in America. Funny that!)

I actually had this exchange once: A guy asked me "What do I do when I'm out on the trail and the horse just freezes up and won't walk off and I'm stuck miles from home?" I asked "How did you deal with it last time?" He answered: "It's my wife's horse. I took out my cell phone, called her and told her to come get me and her (bleeping) horse." So this chapter, then, is for all troubled riders - but most especially for those who get caught out on the trail with their lover's horse and no cell phone.

Important: Horses that pull this stunt are signaling that they need you to fall back and teach or re-teach some basics. Well-trained horses don't flip you the metaphorical bird. (Duh) You need to dedicate yourself to getting better with your hands and going easier on those reins, to bluff more often than you actually kick and to look for and capitalize upon tiny improvements. (Those teachings are beyond the scope of this chapter.) So, when or if this happens to you, try one of today's quick masking-tape fixes, and make a mental note to spend some genuine training time tomorrow. Your horse's training has sprung a leak - and what I give you today are patches - not long-lasting fixes.

First I'll offer some tips more advanced riders might have heard before. It'll be new to the novice riders, so hang in there, my more accomplished equestrians. I'll finish up by offering a real trick to get your horse moving, one you've probably not heard before. I picked it up from Josh Lyons. It's kinda cool in its simplicity and works on older, stubborn horses as well as the young green ones.

When an older, experienced horse freezes up and won't move off, I think we can chalk that up to stubbornness. Don't you? Shouldn't it be safe to assume that your horse sees you up there kicking, screaming and flailing your arms and realizes you want some kind of movement? Taking a step certainly seems like the logical thing to do. But, well, he doesn't care. Why? Because you have a horse that, as John Lyons has said many times, has learned that you give him the devil whether he's standing or moving. So, all things considered, he might as well just stand there. Besides, if you really think about the physics involved in your kicking, you'd realize that you're really not delivering much "oopmph" with those kicks anyway. (And sure, spurs will get them moving - but perhaps a little faster than you'd care for.)

You have two choices with a stopped-up horse: 1) Hit him, 2) Outsmart him. Now, the great problem with #1 (beyond the obvious) is that they can gradually become desensitized and accustomed to "anything you can dish out." Ride enough horses and you'll sooner-rather-than-later find one that will just plain stop and ignore virtually anything you "bring on." (Hello, you appaloosa owners, you!) Then you find yourself in a situation where the only way to make a difference just might border on abuse (and/or, might deliver "too much" movement, as previously mentioned). No, the best way to deal with such a situation is 3) Don't get into this mess in the first place. Get your horse well-schooled in the basics and keep that training consistent. Oh - sorry, I promised quick fixes here... Okay, then let's choose #2, Outsmart the Bugger. Don't sweat this. There's an excellent chance you're smarter than the average horse. To outsmart it you simply have to: Consistently be more stubborn, capitalize on the hand the horse deals you, and consciously build on small improvements.

Something you need to keep in mind here if you're looking for magic in the next few paragraphs: The older the horse is, the longer he's been pulling such shenanigans, the more beginners he's trucked about, the more stubborn he's proven to be in the past, the more any of these experiences factor into this horse's background, the longer it'll take you to make any real difference, let alone put an end to this sort of behavior in such a recalcitrant horse. Worse news still: The more entrenched this bad behavior has become, the harder you'll have to work using the tools I'm about to describe. (Ha-ha. I told you these were quick fixes.) Relax, we'll get you home - but I'm a firm believer in prevention being worth a pound of trips to the emergency ward.

Okay, should you be headed out on the trail (heading away from the barn) and your horse begins to walk ever slower... most likely because he's thinking about heading home to his stall with or without you... and you think there's a good chance he's about to freeze up completely... then try the following: As he next begins to slow up, oblige him by turning 90 degrees back toward the barn. You'll feel him speed up, figuring he's getting his way. (If 90 degrees doesn't speed him up, try 100, 110, etc. but only as much as it takes for him to speed up and travel more openly on his own.) You'll next take a single rein and direct him back a few degrees toward the direction you'd like to go. At this moment, don't think in black and white absolutes. Quit thinking about either going away from the barn or to the barn, instead start moving back and forth like a snake at right angles to the trail. Your job is to get him moving - not to "go down the trail." Moving freely down the trail is a goal, moving smoothly is the immediate task at hand. Remember, and this is important, get off his mouth, quit kicking and RELAX anytime he improves by even one half of one percent.

Something to consider: The same horse that wants to drag on the way out, most likely will want to race the others home. So, that's actually two things that need to be fixed and in a way you're addressing the "sluggish walk away from the barn" by focusing on the "race home" behavior.

Make your corrections when you're moving at a 90 degree angle relative to the trail. Use that time to teach. He'll be far more likely to react positively to your kicks when not directed 180 degrees away from where he'd really rather be. Concentrate on fluid motion and kick or correct only when you feel a slower "noticeable change of leg speed." Walk (or trot) a slalom pattern, like a skier and try to put some life, electricity and rhythm into your travel.

Two hints: A) As you create your slalom pattern, you may find that he really slows down if you turn him from left to right by turning him away from the barn. Experiment and try turning him in the direction of home in order to make use of his natural impulsion. Do what it takes to "get smooth." B) Try this work at a trot if you feel safe doing so. Walking through this work runs the risk of a "bog down," with the two of you moving slower and slower. Don't ever forget: The energy you put into your ride is the energy you'll get out of your ride.

Also, be very aware that once you begin kicking, you're locked into kicking at that strength at that same pace from now until something hot freezes over or he moves. So think before you kick and pick your battles carefully. As previously stated, your job now is to get the horse moving smoothly - in any direction - in a controlled manner and to capitalize on that: When he moves fluidly, you try turning him a degree or two away from the barn. When he slows up, you move him a degree or two back toward the barn. (Remember, he's supposed to be moving at a steady pace - speeding up when turning toward the barn is as obnoxious as dragging himself away from it. It just happens to help us out here, as we use his little "stunt" against him.) Basically, you've gotta be more stubborn than the horse. It doesn't take them long to recognize an inexperience rider, right? Well, it doesn't take the savvy horse long to realize when you've got his number either.

As an aside: Sorry to tell you, but if you're thinking "But my rider friends are moving away and it's only my horse that wants to stop. Dick, Jane and Sally won't wait for me to train." Uh, sorry - get more understanding friends or stay in the arena till you get this licked. You're putting yourself in a dangerous situation if you force the horse through this. Take the time to deal with this correctly and your insurance agent will thank me.

Here's a very big warning: This chapter addresses horses that stop moving on flat and even ground, not horses that balk when asked to cross something like water or a downed tree. To train a horse to cross obstacles one would borrow many of these concepts - but this is no time to mix and match; you may very likely end up sitting in that water.

Okay, next situation: What do we do with the horse that has already frozen up and won't budge? We're miles from home and the batteries are dead in the cell phone and heck, we don't have the number for that guy's wife anyway. First, we'll try the age-old method of pulling the horse's head off to the side. This is classic. Now, it bears stating again that this is more quick-fix than "what's proper." We John Lyons trainers are not big on simply pulling the head to the side on a horse that's not moving. Ideally, you never turn the horse's head without a corresponding change in the horse's legs (either in direction or speed or both). The reasoning is that if you simply move the head (without the feet) then very quickly the connection you've worked so hard to establish between that rein and the horse's leg begins to dissipate. You want to instill "I pick up the rein, you do this with your feet." You don't want to pick up the rein and the horse does... nothing. We're describing a special situation here, though where your legs are burnt out and you're beyond exasperated, so I'm willing to look away... just this once.

All you'll do is simply pick up the rein and pull the horse's head off to one side or the other by a few inches, let's say four. Don't start by wrenching his head to your knee - because where would you go from there if you need to send a more pointed message? (Besides, such a sharp angle makes it exceedingly difficult for him to move so you'd be creating a bigger obstacle.) Start by pulling his head off to the side a bit, bring the rein against your leg to aid your leverage and wait there as if you've got all day. (You just might.) Wait long enough and what you'll (most likely) feel first, is the horse shifting his weight in order to take a step. The millisecond you feel the horse make this shift he's decided to move - so let go of the reins, thrust those hips forward (yours) and try to ride out of your morass. Really believe you're gonna go someplace. Of course, you may go absolutely nowhere - but a positive attitude will be read by your horse. It makes no difference if he moves but a quarter of an inch or even leans forward - it only matters that you reward the correct thought.

Now, you might try giving him a good swift kick should he slow down immediately in an effort to keep the sucker moving - but more of a hard "squeeze-and-release" will probably get you further. Use your best judgment, but usually in situations like this you'll find it most expedient to more or less coax the horse, (I didn't say "Become a patsy"), as opposed to sort of man-handling him with a lot of kicking. If you can get the horse consistently shifting his weight, build on that. Experiment to see what it takes to get the shift to become a "lean" and the lean to become a step taken. This simple method can often fix a horse simply because they soon realize that anytime they stop, you counter with the above. More often than not, you only have to repeat this half a dozen times or so and they'll just walk off as you ask, having learned that the freezing up gets them nowhere (literally).

Another caveat: Be careful not to pull so hard on the reins or in such a direction as to cause the horse to become off-balanced. Try lesser, wider angles. Try using less pressure and more patience. If you find yourself in a situation (using any of the methods described here on these pages) where the little voice in your head says there's a chance the horse might trip over himself, and land on top of you, let go. Live to fight another day. Really, it ain't worth it. Get off and lead the horse home.

Which leads me to a fix that you might try if you've got a horse that stops and you really believe no amount of kicking or rein finagling will every dislodge him: Pick up the rein and add pressure as described, (just a few pounds worth, your knuckles should not be white). Again, lock the rein against a part of your body or the saddle to gain leverage. Wait till the horse parks against your hold and... get off as safely as possible, (watch those stirrups!) being careful to keep the pressure steady as you dismount. Once you're off, hold your pressure steady until you get the horse moving from the ground. (Stand at the point of his left shoulder to stay in a safer area, should he decide to push with a shoulder or kick.) You can pull on the rein by walking backwards away from him then sidestepping to your right; you can smack his butt with your hat, use your imagination - but get the horse's feet and shoulders unlocked. Move him about on the ground, quickly school him on the concept of "pressure and release," then hop back up. You're smarter getting off any horse that you see is becoming a super pill and moving him about (schooling him) on the ground. This is a workable fix because it's win-win. The horse eventually does get moving; it's quick, you've kept your pressure so he never avoided that, you stayed safe - and your neighbors didn't get to see you wailing on Ol' Dobber like a mad man.

I've described the mechanics of building thoughts into leans into steps into full-fledged walking - so I'll be able to breeze through this final cool fix from horseman Josh Lyons, as it makes use of the same concepts.

All you have to do is this: On a horse that's balking and mulishly refusing to move, try applying even pressure with both hands (just enough to let him know you're there and want something). (Don't try this on a horse that might come up on you.) Lock your fists behind the saddle for leverage and wait. Timing is critical: When the horse acts as if he's trying to petulantly thrust his head out and forward, suddenly (and very quickly) push your hands forward (coinciding with his pull), simultaneously allowing the reins to drop out of your hands and squeeze-release with your legs. Turn the power he puts into pulling his head forward into forward momentum for his entire body. Think of it as a child's toy, where the swinging motion of the head pulls the rest of the body forward. Beyond the toy-mechanic physics, this procedure also makes use of a little reverse psychology: Five minutes before, we had a horse who stubbornly refused to move. We replace that "I'm not moving and you can't make me" thought with "If you pull on my head, I can easily walk out of it." Genius! As with the other quick fixes for the stubborn horse described above, make sure you consciously look for - and build on - small improvements from your horse.

Leading Stubborn Horses

Learn a quick fix to get a horse moving again if he freezes up when being led -- with an eye toward lasting changes.

How many times have you begun to lead your horse through a gate, only to have him freeze up a few steps before it? Or maybe he stalls out while you're leading him, plants his front feet and refuses to take one more step? Does he do these things? Uh-oh. Remember "You ride the horse you lead," so stubbornness and attitude in situations like this suggests that you have bigger problems than you might think. Let's fix these things -- but let's also begin seeing them for what they are: Warning signs.

If your horse doesn't walk with you smoothly and willingly, if he drags on that lead rope or otherwise thumbs his nose at you, he is -- simply put -- not broke. You need to deal with it right then and there. (This goes for young and old, green or experienced.) If you're leading your horse out to the arena, trail or what-have-you to ride -- and your horse balks -- and you ignore it -- then not only have you missed an opportunity to improve your relationship with your horse, you've ignored potential danger. Your horse has just told you "I'll go along with you only so far." Worse, he's told you he's ready to rebel to get his way. It doesn't take a genius to see that such rebellions (whether in the horse's mind or acted out in the real world) can lead to some major doctor bills.

Now, don't get me wrong, balking is part of horse ownership for a variety of reasons and to be expected. A few examples: Leaving a horse out in the pasture for any length of time is going to dull his manners. Young horses are going to test you repeatedly in new and unfamiliar situations (a new trail course, his first show, etc.). Experienced lesson horses are going to test novice riders and so on. Even the well-trained show horse of the most accomplished equestrian is going to test the boundaries occasionally. It's natural in the same way that we drive 36 in a 35 mph zone, (until we see the officer holding the speed gun, of course). Horses, like human teens, will test you daily. What matters is not that they do this; what matters is how you handle the incident and with what consistency.

Whether a horse behaves in a poor manner chronically, or just when he's having a bad day, infractions must be corrected straight away and in a thoughtful manner. Neglect to properly address the behavior and you reward the behavior. Then it becomes repeated, practiced and finally habit. This does not mean that we need to go nuts and beat or otherwise scare our horse into cardiac arrest when he pulls a stunt because making an issue out of something now only makes it harder on both of you later. It happens like this: The horse looks at the gate and imagines something bad is going to happen should he walk through it. He balks. You lose your temper and chase him screaming and flailing for twenty minutes. The horse then has proof, "I was right. Bad things do happen at that gate." Your molehill has just become a mountain. Instead, we deal with issues immediately; we're consistent and we're calm.

First a warning: No matter what, do not stand in front of your horse (the horse that won't move) in such a way that he could run into you (or over you), should he come unglued and lurch forward. Keep to the side, at the horse's shoulder. Also, be conscious to place your weight so that you can jump away, should he come at you unexpectedly. When I work near a horse I don't trust, I keep one hand on the horse, (against his shoulder, for instance) not to stop him, but because it tells my brain sooner "The horse has moved. Watch out."

Whether you own a horse that's a proven brat to lead -- or you're working with a youngster, begin to see yourself as a living pinball when the two of you are walking together. That is to say, challenge yourself to keep "rolling" fluidly regardless of what obstacles you might encounter: In the same way that the pinball doesn't freeze up and stop when it hits something (it abruptly changes course and rolls on), you need to concentrate on perpetual movement. Keeping his feet moving in a business-like way (and without pain) teaches him respect for you as leader and pays dividends later on the trail, in the arena or when just hanging out grooming. If your horse balks, get it moving again smoothly and immediately. That means any foot, in any direction. So, if I've described your situation (balky horse or young horse that's learning to lead), do this: Lead your horse from Point A to Point B -- and tell yourself before taking that first step, that the two of you will be in perpetual motion (using the simple methods I'll describe below) until you remove the halter. That simple exercise alone will open your eyes to leaks in your horse's training or your methods.

How do we get the horse moving forward when he refuses to take another step? By getting his rear end moving. That's his motor; use it to get movement and break the stalemate. Forget trying to pull him forward, he'll only dig in deeper. Instead, ask him to move those back legs sideways (away from you): Bring his head off slightly to one side with pressure on the lead line. (You don't want him to gain strength and lasting power by lining up his skeletal structure.) Cluck to him. If that doesn't get those legs moving, try waving your arm toward his rear. If that doesn't work, take up the end of your lead rope and whirl it (away from your horse so as not to startle it into jumping on top of you if you've got a super-nervous horse out there). Whirl it ever closer and if still nothing, whack him on the butt. Did you notice how I didn't say "Start by whacking him on the butt"? Always test the waters for two reasons: 1) You want the horse to work on less, that is, to move when you cluck; you don't want to have to smack him each time and 2) The horse might react to "the smack from nowhere" by knocking you on the floor. Start small. You can always add pressure.

A special note: Have you noticed how I haven't prescribed "forcing the horse to move backwards with jerks on the lead rope"? That's because all this manages to accomplish is to train the horse to throw his head up, stretch out his front feet, arch his back and move backwards with zero agility, still scared.

So when you can move your horse's hips, get those shoulders unlocked. In the same way that you can divert the flow of water out various leaks in a hose by crimping the hose, we'll apply pressure and ask the horse to move -- and we'll keep applying that pressure until that energy finds its way to his shoulders. Stand at the horse's left shoulder, facing him, lead rope in your left hand about 6 inches below his jaw. Ask his hind end to move (to his right, your left) as you've done. As he steps off, change your focus to his shoulders and ask them to move (also to his right, your left), by kissing, twirling the rope in his direction, applying ever greater pressure. Make him understand that he needs to keep moving and to keep trying to find the answer ("Move your hind end AND your shoulders"). He can only move x-many body parts y-many directions so he'll figure this out pretty quick, they always do. Be patient.

When you first begin, release and pet when he even leans in the proper direction. Release if he lifts himself or shuffles his feet as if to move the shoulders. Release if you think he's even thinking of moving those shoulders. Learn to build (through the timing of your release) on these small improvements and soon he'll be moving solidly (and directly) to the side.

Before you know it, you'll have the horse easily sidestepping his hips and shoulders fluidly and evenly, in either direction, together or individually. Back away and get your movement at some distance, maybe six feet, twirling your lead line, asking the horse to side step left, then right. When he'll move lightly sideways, as if skating on ice, you'll find that he'll obligingly walk forward as well. He'll also move back if you follow this sequence with no hesitations: Ask him to move sideways (away from you), then forward, then solely his hips and then finally backwards. He'll drop his head lower than before, not push on the lead rope, lift his belly and bow slightly away from you through the center of his body. Practice this and give it a shot anytime your horse drags on that lead. He'll soon be reminded that it's far easier to simply walk forward pleasantly.

Tips:

1) As goofy as it sounds, horses are prey animals and they can really tell what part of their body you're staring at. If you want to move the hip, pick a small part of that hip and stare at it, doing what it takes to "move that spot." This will also serve to keep you focused on the simple task at hand.

2) Do your very best to move as little as possible while practicing this. When I teach this, I probably never move off a space the size of a briefcase. Sure, I move (pivot) when necessary, but it's not a matter of moving several feet in any one direction. Tell yourself, "If he can do it, so can I."

3) Remember, once you apply pressure (to the reins or the lead rope), any lightening of your pull, however slight, could reward the horse at the wrong time. Be very careful to keep even pressure (even if you have to carefully swap hands as you reposition yourself) until the horse earns a proper release.

4) Always know what you're going to do if the horse flatly refuses a request and you find yourself stalemated. Case in point, this is what you've been doing when the horse refuses to budge and you react by immediately getting the hind end to move. Rather than face a deadlock, (and, hence, reward the horse) you got the rear moving. Another example might be when you're trying to teach the horse to walk backwards or to move his shoulders. If he parks out and won't do either, you can react by saying "Fine, then move your back end." Disengaging that big old fat butt is hard work -- and you'll find that it often pays off as a great motivator if the horse refuses your initial request to do something else.

5) Don't forget the horse needs to practice each maneuver from both the left and right sides. Expect him to be better on one than the other -- and compensate for this by spending more time on the weaker side.

6) If your horse tries throwing up his head and crowding you with it (and they try this frequently), then shove your hand (the one closest to his head) high into the air, towards his ear as if a school student throwing his hand into the air for the teacher. The sudden movement will back him off and tell him he's made a mistake.

7) If your horse just parks out, that is, he won't move his shoulders or won't move period, then you're not applying enough pressure to his butt. You need the horse to be thinking "move." Use common sense here, but remember, the energy you put in is often the energy the horse puts out. In other words, if you go to sleep, don't be surprised if your horse does as well.

8) Wanna test yourself and your horse? Bring your horse's body parallel to a large gate and slowly, very slowly, swing the gate toward your horse. If you've properly trained your horse, you should be able to hold his head steady as his front and back legs sidestep smoothly and evenly away from that gate.

Picking Up Feet

Teaching your horse to lift its feet on command is actually much simpler than folks tend to want to make it. Here's how.

Teaching our horses to pick up their feet is only "hard" when we try to force the horse to do so right this moment rather than taking (any rational amount of) time to do some proper training. It seems so simple to us. "Just pick up your darn feet and stand there, dummy." Well, think of it from your prey animals point of view: Attaching any single part of his body to something, you, for instance, means that he can't run away. Every chromosome in his thousand pound body says this is the last thing you do. If you have no way to tell the horse to stand still or to relax, if you haven't spent the time to gain the horse's trust, you're asking for a frustrating and dangerous experience.

(I will assume that all four of your horse's legs are sound as you begin this -- heaven help you if you try to teach a rebel to lift its right hind leg when there's an abscess in the front left.)

Before tackling this topic, make absolutely sure that your horse has been thoroughly sacked out to your touch. If that little voice says there is any way your horse is going to react negatively (flinch, freeze up, pull away, try to kick, etc.) to your touch, especially when working around those back feet, then... you ain't ready. Conversely, if that little voice says "All systems go," then you should have an easy day of it.

You can teach the following very simply without a round pen -- but the round pen offers two significant advantages: 1) You don't have to juggle a lead line in one hand, and 2) Should the horse need a little extra motivation to play along, you can send him around a few rotations.

The better we can control the hind end of the horse, the easier it is to control the front half of the horse. So, we start with the back feet. Standing on the horse's left side, you'll ask the rear of the horse to move away. Ask him to take a step or two and when he stops, look at the back leg closest to you (the one we'd like to pick up). Does he have any weight on it? We want to keep asking him to move, then pausing, then asking him to move until, by chance, he stands with that nearest back leg cocked up. You've seen this stance a million times. They'll stand there with weight on three feet, the fourth resting, slightly turned up, toe to heel.

If he comes to a stop with the leg cocked, allow him to stand there and pet him. If not, get him moving again immediately. Be relaxed about it, this is no time for tense. This initial step might take 10, 20, 30 or even more attempts before the horse happens upon the correct answer. (And you may very well think it impossible in the interim.) But once he figures out the pattern and release, he'll quickly learn and begin consistently shifting the weight off the leg at your request. If he puts the weight back on the foot, just move him again until he keeps that leg slightly raised, heel off the ground.

Begin petting the horse's head, gradually working your way back to the hindquarters. When you have "petted your way" back to the hind leg, place your hand on the back of the lower part of the leg and see if you can't "suggest" that it lift off the ground an inch or two. Let it drop on its own, pat your way back to the head. Repeat this process, gradually asking for more, moving and repositioning the horse anytime he goes "flatfooted" on you. Try your level-best to release the foot a beat before you think he's about to pull it away. Convince him that handing over his foot is not a forever thing.

When you let go of the horse's foot, you should do just that: Let go. If the foot drops a time or two, he'll quickly learn to hold it himself, rather than developing the annoying habit of placing more and more weight on you. Being overly concerned about our horse's balance is a major cause of leaning. Trust me, he doesn't want to tip over and is more than capable of standing squarely, so to speak, on three feet. If the horse knows that you can and will drop his foot at any time, he'll be careful to not place weight on that foot.

To train those front feet, stand on your horse's left side and simply press on his shoulder, in effect, pushing him directly away. You don't have to apply that much pressure, just enough to be rather annoying, sending a clear signal that you're looking for something. That something is just this: "Horse, shift your weight to the opposite foot." Remember that a lowly fly can cause your horse to move by landing on a lip and being irritating enough, so practice patience. If your horse leans into your press, then ask the back legs to disengage (shoulder stays put, hips move away), then ask again. Moving that four hundred pound butt is work, so this (disengagement) is a terrific motivator. The movement also helps transfer some of the weight to the back half of the horse.

Repeat the process you used for the back legs, asking the horse to transfer most of his weight to the opposite foot, moving him anytime he shifts back incorrectly. Pet his head, working your way down to the foot, then back to the head or the shoulders. Before long you'll be able to (by lifting the hoof) lift the horse's foot. Be careful to release before he tries to take it back. The last thing you want is to cowboy through this with a tug of war. It won't be long before your body language, your bending at the waist and lean against the horse's shoulders, will become your cue for the horse to lift his leg. As usual, you'll need to repeat this sequence on the right side of the horse.

You'll notice that farriers ask your horse to place its legs in positions that must seem truly bizarre to the young horse. We riders pick up the leg, clean it and we're done. Farriers hold feet for longer periods of time, bend legs into more exaggerated positions -- and make more noise than fifty garbage cans tumbling down a metal staircase. Practice with your horse, using patience and repetition to be ready for your first shoeing. Ask to hold the foot for increasingly longer periods of time, at "odder angles." Bring the leg up, between your own legs as the farrier does. Tap on the foot with a rock, bang the occasional feed bucket, maybe throw in a sporadic "Aagh, my aching back" if you're looking for true realism.

Teaching your horse to next lift its feet by simply pointing is more than a neat trick. Recall how the horse learns to lean on us: We lift the leg, offering 2, 5, or 10 pounds of support and he quickly learns to lean with 3, 6 or 11 pounds. When you expect less, you get less. Expect the horse to lift his own leg and never get into this situation.

Take a dressage whip, kiss (to say "move something") and tap the inside of the horse's front leg, near the "knee joint" until the horse bends his leg, shifting his weight. Pet him and repeat the process. Each time he advances his understanding, ask for a bit more "of a lift." If he stalls out at a certain height, don't stop your tapping, keep at it until the leg moves higher. You might try taking your lead rope and wrapping it very loosely (so that it would drop off should he walk off) around the very bottom of his leg. Apply a little pressure to this rope, suggesting that he lift his leg as you kiss then tap. This often helps speed up the process. Also, when you tap, hold your arm and dressage whip as if you're pointing. When the horse consistently lifts his foot to the tap, drop the whip, but hold out your arm as if still carrying it. Kiss and move your arm as if tapping. Of course, the first few times you'll need to revert to using the whip to back up your request -- but that's where a light tug on the rope can help out. Be careful to look for very slight improvement at first, maybe he just shifts his weight or bends at the knee. Reward every little improvement and your horse will soon be lifting his leg following a kiss and a point.

You'll use the same system to work your way around the horse, teaching the concept to all four feet. Note that if you start with the front left foot, then move to the front right, you might be surprised to find that your kiss and point cue doesn't mean "lift the leg I point at." Instead, it'll mean (to your horse) "lift the front left leg." They just don't make the transference in their brain as we might (like to) expect. You'll need to train each leg individually. And it can get pretty funny as you work your way around. Your horse will typically resort to doing what got it a release the last time you made a similar request. So, when you first begin with the fourth leg, he might very well lift all of the other three before that fourth leg. It'll look like he's dancing and the fact is, if you want to take this a step further and teach your horse "to dance," this is exactly how you'd do it. Point to one then the other in quick succession.

When your horse understands "lift that leg when I point to it," begin moving back at an angle to that foot. Kiss and point at a two foot distance, then three and so on. Before long you'll be able to stand thirty feet away, "at your horse's four corners," and cause him to lift that particular leg on command. Pretty neat for a horse that wouldn't lift his feet at all for you just a day before, right?

Picking Up Feet

Books by This Author

Check out these titles from Keith Hosman

- Crow Hopper's Big Guide to Buck Stopping
- Get On Your Horse: Curing Mounting Problems
- Horse Tricks
- How to Start a Horse: Bridling to 1st Ride
- Rein In Your Horse's Speed
- Round Penning: First Steps to Starting a Horse
- Trailer Training
- What I'd Teach Your Horse (Basic Training)
- What Is Wrong with My Horse? (Problem Solving)
- When Your Horse Rears... How to Stop It
- Your Foal: Essential Training

Available in all major formats, including:

Paperback | Kindle | Nook | PDF | Kobo | Apple

Purchase 24/7 at Horsemanship101.com/Courses

What Is Wrong with My Horse?

Meet the Author

Keith Hosman, John Lyons Certified Trainer

Keith Hosman lives just outside of San Antonio, Texas and divides his time between writing how-to training materials and conducting training clinics in most of these United States as well as in Germany and the Czech Republic.

Visit his flagship site horsemanship101.com for more D.I.Y. training and to find a clinic happening soon near you.

How-to articles & trainer listings: horsemanship101.com

Printed in Great Britain
by Amazon